Church, Law and Political Transition in Malawi 1992 — 1994

Edited by
Matembo S. Nzunda and Kenneth R. Ross

MAMBO PRESS
in association with
UNIVERSITY OF MALAWI
Religious & Theological Studies Department

MAMBO PRESS
P.O. Box 779, Gweru, Zimbabwe
Tel: 263 — 54 — 4016/7
Fax: 263 — 54 — 51991

Die Deutsche Bibliothek - CIP Einheitsaufnahme

CHURCH, LAW AND POLITICAL TRANSITION IN MALAWI
1992 —1994
M. S. Nzunda, Kenneth R. Ross (Hrsg)
Bonn: Verl. für Kultur und Wiss., 1995
        (Kachere series: Bd 1)
ISBN   3 926105 41 0
NE: Nzunda, Matembo S (Hrsg) OT

Mambo Press/Gweru/Zimbabwe/Africa
ISBN   0 86922 602 9

First Published 1995

Printed and published in Zimbabwe
by Mambo Press, Senga Road, Gweru
1995

Contents

Contributors

Gracian Z. Banda is a Lecturer in Law in the Department of Law, University of Malawi. He holds a Master of Laws degree in International Economic Law from the University of Warwick, UK.

J.C. Chakanza is Senior Lecturer and Head of the Department of Theology and Religious Studies in the University of Malawi. He received his doctorate from the University of Oxford. He is the author of many articles and the editor of *Religion in Malawi*. Fr Chakanza also serves as Catholic Chaplain to the University of Malawi.

Robert M. Nkhalambayausi Chirwa is a Lecturer in Computer Science in the Department of Mathematical Sciences, University of Malawi. He was awarded a Masters degree in Computer Science by the University of Kentucky in 1990. He has contributed papers to recent conferences on Information Technology in Southern Africa.

Klaus Fiedler lectures in church history and missiology in the Department of Theology and Religious Studies, University of Malawi. He holds doctorates from the University of Dar-es-Salaam in Tanzania and the University of Heidelberg in Germany. The author of many publications, his major work is *The History of the Faith Missions* (Oxford: Regnum, 1994). He is also the editor of the German missiological journal *Evangelikale Missiologie*.

Fidelis Kanyongolo is a Lecturer in Law at the University of Malawi. As a student he was detained without trial in Mikuyu Prison for one year. He is active in human rights work in Malawi.

Fulata Lusungu Moyo is currently teaching at Masongola Secondary School in Zomba. She holds a B.Ed. from the University of Malawi, an Honours degree and a Masters degree in Religious Studies from the University of Zimbabwe, and a Certificate in Ecumenical Studies from the Ecumenical Institute, University of Geneva. She has contributed to *Religion in Malawi*.

Anthony J.M. Nazombe is a Senior Lecturer in the Department of English, University of Malawi. He has a doctorate in English Literature from the University of Sheffield, UK. He is editor of the anthology *The Haunting Wind: New Poetry from Malawi* (Blantyre: Dzuka, 1990). He is also the current Vice Chairperson of the

Association of Teachers of Literature and Language (ATOLL), a SADC organisation.

Peter Ngulube-Chinoko is a teacher at Katoto Secondary School in Mzuzu and a part-time M.A. student in the Department of Theology and Religious Studies, University of Malawi. As an undergraduate he was expelled from the same University after publishing poems which were considered to be too critical of the government. He was able to continue his studies in Rome and was awarded a B.A. with distinction.

Matembo S. Nzunda is a Senior Lecturer in the Department of Law, University of Malawi. He holds a doctorate in Company Law from the University of Cambridge in England. He has published numerous papers on various aspects of the law, including company law, conflict of laws and environmental law. He also practises law in Malawi. At the 1994 General Election he was elected as the Alliance for Democracy M.P. for Chitipa North.

Kenneth R. Ross is a Senior Lecturer in the Department of Theology and Religious Studies, University of Malawi. He was awarded a doctorate in ecclesiastical history by the University of Edinburgh in 1987. He is the author of *Church and Creed in Scotland* (Edinburgh: Rutherford, 1988) and has written many articles on church history and theology. He is the current Secretary of the Association of Theological Institutions in Southern and Central Africa (ATISCA).

James Tengatenga is an Anglican priest and a lecturer in Systematic and Pastoral Theology at Zomba Theological College.

1. Introduction

Matembo S. Nzunda and Kenneth R. Ross

The two year span between the issue of the Catholic bishops' pastoral letter of March 1992 and the General Election of May 1994 has been marked by a process of rapid political change in Malawi. To find comparable turning points in earlier history it is necessary to look to the imposition of British colonial rule in 1889–1891 or the achievement of independence in 1962–64. Though it is still too early to assess how the present transition will compare with these social revolutions, it is clear already that the political landscape has been transformed. The last two years have seen the shaking and then the dismantling of the apparatus of the one–party state. From 1964 to 1992 there was no serious challenge mounted from within Malawi to the total control of Dr Hastings Kamuzu Banda and his Malawi Congress Party government. Though the early 1990s brought signs that the climate was changing, few were prepared for the bombshell of the Lenten pastoral letter issued by the Roman Catholic bishops on 8 March 1992. Quite suddenly the truth about the oppression and exploitation of the Malawi system was clearly stated. It was immediately apparent that the issue of the letter was an epoch–making event and that the government faced the most serious challenge of its 30 years in office.

Within weeks students and workers had organised strikes, hitherto unheard of, to voice their demands for liberalization. Chakufwa Chihana, a prominent trade unionist, returned from a conference in Lusaka, to announce publicly his commitment to campaign for democracy and human rights in Malawi. Though immediately arrested and detained Chihana became a symbol, both internationally and within Malawi, of the need for radical political reform in the country. These opposition forces were strengthened by the decision of the international donor community, at its meeting in Paris in May 1992, to suspend development aid to Malawi until its record on human rights and good governance was improved. Internally a powerful engine for reform emerged with the formation of the Public Affairs Committee (PAC) which was organised by the churches but included representatives of the Muslim community, the Malawi Law Society and the business community. When the President agreed that government ministers should hold discussions with the PAC it was the first time that a non-party organisation had been acknowledged as having a role to play in national political life. The pace of change was quickening. The combination of internal and external pressure finally, in October 1992, forced the government to concede that a national referendum should be held on the question of whether to retain the one-party system or to adopt a multi-party system of government.

Organised opposition now emerged, initially in the form of "pressure groups" campaigning for multi-party democracy. By early 1993 these groups - the Alliance for Democracy (AFORD) and the United Democratic Front (UDF) - were clawing back the freedom of speech and the freedom of assembly which had been denied under MCP rule. These were heady days as many people found themselves, for the first time, free to express their views. A vigorous independent press was formed during this period and immediately attracted an eager readership. After many years of having only two, government-controlled newspapers in which news coverage was largely restricted to MCP propaganda, one of the most visible signs of change was the many newspapers on the streets which offered sharp critique of the prevailing one-party system. Despite a furious rearguard action by the Malawi Congress Party, it was clear that the government was in trouble when vast crowds thronged the opposition rallies while in many areas MCP rallies were subject to a virtual boycott. It was no surprise to most observers when the vote at the national referendum of 14 June 1993 gave a two-thirds majority to the multi-party advocates. Great was the euphoria when the government not only allowed the results to be announced but promised to abide by them.

Clearly the referendum result was a vote of no confidence in the MCP and in President Banda who had identified himself unreservedly with the maintenance of the one-party system. The government, however, resisted calls for its immediate resignation on the basis that it was still constitutionally in office. This position was accepted by the opposition on the understanding that it would obtain only for the transitional period needed for the establishment of the new multi-party system. The victorious opposition demanded its rightful place in this process. Accordingly legislation was soon enacted in Parliament to allow new political parties to register. A cross-party National Consultative Council and National Executive Committee were appointed to oversee the transition to multi-party government. Meanwhile dramatic reforms had been implemented in the area of human rights. Almost all political prisoners had been released, the International Red Cross had been invited to inspect the prisons and a general amnesty was declared to allow all political exiles to return to the country. By the end of the year Parliament had abolished the Life Presidency, detention without trial, the Forfeiture Act and the Decency in Dress Act – all integral parts of the former apparatus of repression. A General Election was called for 17 May 1994. Yet still there were fears that the government might seek to subvert the democratization process. Particular concern surrounded the Malawi Young Pioneers, the armed MCP youth organisation which had been extensively used as an instrument of political control. Though it was made clear that it was not possible in a multi-party system to have one party with an armed wing, the government stalled on the question of disarmament. Finally, in early December some army officers, provoked by the MYP killing of two soldiers, took matters into their own hands and launched the successful "Operation Bwezani" to defeat and disarm the Young Pioneers.

Though some MYP forces fled to Mozambique from where it was feared they might launch raids aimed at destabilization, the MCP's capacity to intimidate the population was greatly reduced. As the General Election campaign got underway in early 1994 there were reports of Nyau traditional dancers being used in an intimidatory way by the MCP in the Central Region. However, when the independent Electoral Commission, chaired by Justice Mrs Anastasia Msosa, took a firm line in condemning such tactics, the practice was largely abandoned. Meanwhile civic education was proving successful and the electorate was well prepared for the polling exercise held on 17 May 1994. With the exception of only two constituencies the voting was found to have been free and fair. Bakili Muluzi of UDF won the Presidential election with 47% of the vote, comfortably ahead of Kamuzu Banda of MCP with 33% and Chakufwa Chihana of AFORD with 19%. Dr Banda graciously conceded defeat and the new President was sworn in on 21 May 1994, the new democratic constitution having been put into effect immediately following the election. Debate on the details of the constitution will continue as particular provision was made for Parliament to enact amendments within the first year. The problem of regionalism will also demand the attention of politicians since the election results revealed that each of the three main parties has overwhelming support in a particular region – UDF in the Southern, MCP in the Central and AFORD in the Northern. Nevertheless, while the political debate continues, it is clear that the successful General Election of May 1994 marks the conclusion of the process of transition to democratic government. This book offers analysis, from mainly legal and theological perspectives, of some key aspects of the political transition.

Resources drawn from both theology and law proved to be of decisive significance in Malawi's "peaceful revolution." Of course, there were certainly strictly political reasons for the changes which occurred. The change in the international climate in 1989–90, together with the internal contradictions which became apparent in the MCP regime, gave an unprecedented opportunity for organised opposition to emerge. Yet, at the same time, there was an unmistakable religious component to the "Malawi revolution". It was the pastoral letter of the Catholic bishops which actually ignited the fires of protest. Both in the composition of the letter and in standing firm under intense government pressure to withdraw the statement, it is clear that the bishops drew deeply on the resources of their Christian faith. That same faith offered inspiration to numerous preachers over the following few months to echo in their pulpits the prophetic critique advanced by the pastoral letter. This was still extremely dangerous and such preachers were subject to threats, harassment and, sometimes, detention. Especially in the early period of March–September 1992 it was in the context of the church that people found the courage to raise their voices in protest. The influential Presbyterian Synods of Blantyre and Livingstonia rallied behind the call of the Catholic bishops and it was the Presbyterians who were largely responsible for the process which led to the formation of the Public Affairs Committee which was to become the engine of political reform in 1992–93. In 1993 the churches proved to be probably the most effective agents of voter education in the run–up to the referendum. Certainly the opposition of the churches was a key factor in the downfall of the one-party system. Following the referendum the churches remained engaged with the ongoing political process. A feature of this period was the foundation of human rights "desks" in a number of church organisations as the church sought to establish a watchdog role in relation to the future political life of the country. A good deal of the power of the reform movement came from the inspiration which church members derived from their faith. This was acknowledged by President Muluzi when he began his inaugural address by thanking the church leaders for "showing the way" and urged them to continue offering guidance to the political process.[1]

From an early stage the democratization movement had also expressed itself in legal terms. The Government seemed to have sensed the challenge as early as the first half of 1991 when women in urban areas began to wear dress banned by the dressing law of 1973. A number of women were arrested, tried, convicted and sentenced to pay fines. The police expressed outrage in the newspapers, threatening to punish any person who violated the dress law. When one of the monthly magazines published a letter challenging the police interpretation of the law the letter writer and the editor were immediately arrested, threatened with sedition charges and released the following day. Thus began the debate on the dress law ending in its repeal in December, 1993.

The official response to student protests led to the dismissal of 11 students at Chancellor College. They took the University to court. In the first ruling of this kind in Malawi the High Court reversed the dismissal and ordered the reinstatement of the students. The ruling and the newspapers were quick to condemn the University decision. In ordering the reinstatement of the students, the court passed the message to the public in Malawi that it had become possible not to be punished, without first being tried, for mounting political protests.

In 1992 the increasing need for political thinking to express itself led to the launching of the *The Malawi Democrat* in Zambia and *UDF News* in Malawi. The Government felt threatened by this freedom of expression and the freedom of opinion expressed in the plays of Du Chisiza, Jr. The newspapers and the staging of plays in schools were banned by the Ministers of Justice and of Education. Applications were made to the High Court for Judicial review of the bans. All the applications were successful and the bans were lifted. Thus, the law helped in the process of change by creating an environment in which arbitrary Ministerial decisions which stood in the way of change were struck down.

---

1 See, e.g., *The Nation*, Vol. 1 No. 37, 23 May 1994.

The quickening of administrative law was not matched by criminal law. After the pastoral letter there followed a spate of anonymous fax messages directed against some political figures in the country. The police preferred sedition charges against suspects but awaited the result of the Chihana trial. The issue in this case was simple: do words, however strong they may be, directed against the President and his Government amount to sedition if they do not disclose an intention by the speaker, writer or publisher to incite violence? The High Court and the Supreme Court of Appeal answered "Yes". This answer was against the trend set by the courts themselves in administrative law. However, the Chihana trial had three positive results. One is that the Supreme Court of Appeal ruled that the United Nations Universal Declaration of Human Rights is part of the domestic law of Malawi. A second is that the trial showed that there were still some people in Malawi who were able and willing to risk their lives for the sake of others in Malawi. It also proved that the law of sedition at the time was heavily weighted in favour of the authoritarian status quo and led to the change of the law in December 1993.

In order to take account of these important developments in national life the Department of Law and the Department of Theology and Religious Studies at the Chancellor College of the University of Malawi joined forces at the beginning of the 1993–94 academic year to organise a series of seminars which would examine different aspects of the transition. Three weekend meetings were held between October 1993 and March 1994. The papers presented at these seminars form the basis for this book. It was soon apparent to the 150 or so students and staff who participated in the seminars that the material being generated could be beneficial to a much wider audience. This gave us the confidence that we could offer an in–depth analysis of some significant aspects of the transition which could be of assistance to those working for a better Malawi as well as to interested observers seeking a clearer understanding of recent developments.

In the first essay Matembo Nzunda draws on his experience as defence lawyer in Chakufwa Chihana's sedition trial to offer a study of Malawi's sedition laws within the framework of social contract theory. He shows that in Malawian history, contrary to the expectations of incumbent governments, the use of the criminal law has not been an effective means of obstructing the renegotiation of the terms of the social contract. Kenneth Ross attempts to identify the distinctive resources on which the churches were able to draw in their engagement with Malawian politics during 1992–93. He argues that it is as the churches themselves undergo transformation that they become effective agents of social change. The strikes and riots of May 1992 marked the re-emergence of organised labour as a force on the Malawian political scene. Gracian Banda takes up this long–suppressed subject and argues for the importance of labour securing the freedom to organise and bargain collectively. Joseph Chakanza places the celebrated Lenten pastoral letter in the context of Catholic social witness and draws some illuminating comparisons with Malawi's earlier history. "Edge" Kanyongolo addresses the question of censorship in light of the demise of the totalitarian system. His essay has already been acknowledged to be an important contribution to the debate on the reform of the censorship laws. Peter Ngulube–Chinoko draws on personal observations and interviews to paint a grim picture of the experience of women under the one–party state. Yet he argues that women made key contributions to the political transition and opens up a discussion of their future role in Malawian political life.

The transition as a whole was remarkably peaceful but there were two days which seemed very much like war – when the Malawi Army set about "disarming" the Young Pioneers. James Tengatenga argues that the violence used in "Operation Bwezani" can be justified from the standpoint of Christian ethics. One of the first signs of impending political change in 1992 was the appearance of fax messages critical of the MCP government. Robert Chirwa argues that the development of information technology in Malawi at least hastened the demise of the totalitarian system of control imposed under one–party rule. Fulata Moyo takes a critical look at the social witness of the renowned Livingstonia Synod of the Church of Central Africa Presbyterian. She argues that the Synod has still to discover real integrity in its prophetic ministry to the nation. Anthony Nazombe provides an incisive analysis of perhaps the two most important books of poetry to appear during the transition, by Steve Chimombo and Jack Mapanje. This literary critique highlights some of the important nuances of the politics of the transition. Klaus Fiedler, in the final essay, assesses the contribution of the "smaller" churches to political change in Malawi. He argues that, although often neglected by scholars, account must be taken of the witness of such churches if we are to give a complete picture of the role of religion in social transformation. The essays, taken together, make no pretence to be comprehensive in their analysis. However, they are offered as one contribution to the formation of a sound understanding of the political transformation experienced in Malawi between 1992 and 1994.

2. Sedition and the Struggle for the Social Contract

Matembo S. Nzunda

1. Introduction

The purpose of criminal law is to protect the social contract which resolves into two related contracts. One is that between a citizen and society and another is that between citizens inter se. Society is represented by the state.

There are three groups of citizens: those who like the terms of the social contract as it is; those who do not like the terms of the contract and seek to renegotiate them; and those who are or appear to be indifferent. Those citizens who manage the state belong to the first group and threaten to or actually use the criminal law with the hope that the second group will temporarily or permanently cease to seek to renegotiate the terms of the social contract. These efforts by the two groups are made to persuade a sufficient number of the third group to stop being or appearing to be indifferent and join either the first or second group. This is what has been called "The struggle for the social contract" (Dahrendorf, 1985). This paper will use two periods in Malawi to show that the first group always fails to use the criminal law to stop a renegotiation of the terms of the social contract.

2. The Struggle for Independence

One of the two periods is that leading to Independence in 1964. One of the main supporters of political change was Henry Chipembere. On 28th November, 1960 and 3rd December, 1960, he made political speeches to large African audiences at Rumphi and Zomba respectively. He was charged with uttering seditious words and of proposing violence. The magistrate's court, the High Court of Nyasaland and the Federal Supreme Court all found him guilty of the offences and sentenced him. The Court said:

> "It is tragic to hear him, as an educated man the victim of
> obsession, ridden by the wholly irrational belief that his pro-
> paganda is true ...." (*Chipembere* at 89 per Clayden, F.C.J.
> quoting the lower court).

The trial, conviction and sentence of Chipembere did not deter supporters of political change from continuing with the struggle. In January and February, 1961 a paper was published in English as the
"Voice of the Malawi Worker" and in Chinyanja as "Umodzi pa
Ntchito". This time the "victim of obsession" was Aleke Banda who
was editor of the paper. He was charged with publishing a seditious
publication. Again, the magistrate's court, the High Court of Nyasaland and the Federal Supreme Court found him guilty of this offence.
Clayden, F.C.J. said:

> "In the February article there was an attack on the Nyasaland
> Police. The words used were clearly seditious and clearly dis-
> played seditious intent in the senses charged": *Banda* at 113

In both *Chipembere* and *Banda* the Law Report does not give extracts
of the words which were used. This is unfortunate on two counts.
First, from the Report, it is impossible to know what changes in the
terms of the social contract the supporters of political change were
urging. However, the history of the struggle for independence in
Malawi shows that change was urged in the following terms of the
social contract. One of them restricted or excluded the right of the
Africans to take part in the government of their country directly or
through freely chosen representatives. A second term of the social
contract divided the sovereignty of the country between Nyasaland
and the Federation of Rhodesia and Nyasaland of which it was a mere
territory. The first term meant that policies would be formulated and
passed into laws which were then interpreted and enforced against
Africans who had taken no direct or representative part in the process
of law making. These laws included that of sedition and were
designed to ensure that political change was put off for as long as
there was no one who was prepared to demonstrate the unfairness of
the terms of the social contract by his ability and willingness to suffer
for it. The second count is that it is impossible to use *Chipembere* and
Banda as authority for the proposition that an intention to incite
violence is not an essential ingredient of the offence of sedition. If
anything, *Chipembere* genuflects in the opposite direction. This will
be dealt with later.

The terms of the social contract as renegotiated between 1960 and 1963 are reflected in the Malawi Independence Order 1964 and the Independence Constitution of that year. The laws made for Malawi and in force before 6th July, 1964 would continue in force. One of such laws was the Penal Code containing the law of sedition. The National Assembly elected during the General Election of 1961 would continue in existence. The force of the law on emergency powers first made in 1939 was going to expire on 6th July, 1966. The Prime Minister would promote localization of the public service by requests for compulsory retirement. The citizens of Malawi would be Africans, Asians and Europeans who met specified descriptions. Every person had guaranteed and justiciable human rights.

The Government was divided into the legislature consisting of Her Majesty and a National Assembly, the Judiciary consisting of the magistracy, the High Court, the Supreme Court of Appeal and the Judicial Committee of the Privy Council. The tenure of judges was firmly protected. A multi-party system of government was not specifically provided for but was part of the freedom of assembly and association and expressly referred to: s.39(2)(e)(5).

The government by constitutional monarchy was altered in 1966 following Constitutional Proposals of 1965. The fundamental change which is reflected in section 1(2) of the 1966 Constitution is that the power to govern the country is no longer derived from Her Majesty but from the consent of the governed. This point must be appreciated because it underpins the struggle of the social contract between the Rulers and the Ruled. The law of sedition contains the rules which regulate that struggle. In favour of the Rulers section 51 bans seditious words, seditious publications and the doing of acts with a seditious intention. And section 50 (1) defines a "seditious intentions" as:

"an intention –
(a) to bring into hatred or contempt or to excite disaffection against the person of the President, or the Government;
(b) to excite the subjects of the President to procure the alteration, otherwise than by lawful means, of any other matter in the Republic; or
(c) to bring into hatred or contempt or to excite disaffection against the administration of justice in the Republic; or
(d) to raise discontent or disaffection among the subjects of the President; or
(e) to promote feeling of ill-will and hostility between different classes of the population of the Republic."

The key active verbs are: bring, excite, promote, raise; and the key nouns are: alteration, contempt, disaffection, discontent, hatred, hostility, ill-will. Thus, there can be the following seditious acts:

(i)	bring into hatred;
(ii)	bring into contempt;
(iii)	excite disaffection;
(iv)	excite alteration;
(v)	promote feeling of ill-will and hostility;
(vi)	raise discontent;
(vii)	raise disaffection.

If this was all there was to the definition of seditious intention the law of sedition would be extremely easy but the democratic struggle of the social contract would be impossible: the Rulers would rule and the Ruled would be ruled without dissent. We would be back in time to the days of King Henry VIII or Shaka Zulu. This is especially so because section 50(2) states that in determining whether the intention with which any act was done, any words were spoken, or any document was published, was or was not seditious

> "every person shall be deemed to intend the consequences which would naturally follow from his conduct at the time and under the circumstances in which he so conducted himself".
> See also *Buchanan* at 527 and *Chihana 1992* at 9-11.

In order to avoid this situation section 50(1) states that an act, speech or publication is not seditious by reason *only* that it intends

> "(i) to show that the President has been misled or mistaken in any of his measures; or
> (ii) to point out errors or defects in the Government or Constitution or in legislation or in the administration of justice with a view to the remedying of such errors or defects;
> (iii) to persuade the subjects of the President to attempt to procure by lawful means the alteration of any matter in the Republic; or
> (iv) to point out with a view to their removal, any matters which are producing or have a tendency to produce feelings of ill-will and enmity between different classes of the population of the Republic".

The key active verbs here are: persuade, point out, procure, remedy, show. Other key words are: alteration, defects, errors, lawful, means, misled, mistaken. These four qualifications to the definition of a seditious intention are intended to promote the democratic struggle of the social contract but put the law of sedition into a dilemma: the promotion of the democratic struggle on the one hand and the maintenance of the *status quo* on the other. The case of Chihana in the High Court of Malawi, *Chihana 1992*, and in the Malawi Supreme Court of Appeal, *Chihana 1993*, is an excellent demonstration of this dilemma.

3. The Struggle for a Better Malawi

The facts as stated in *Chihana 1992* are that the accused left for Zambia on 3rd March, 1992. On his return to Malawi on 6th April, 1992 he was arrested at the airport in Lilongwe while in possession of a number of documents, including the following material ones:

1st: Call for all churches to speak out against Human Rights Abuse in Malawi.

2nd: Malawi: Prospects for Democracy Key-Note Address.

3rd: Address by Chakufwa Chihana on his return to Malawi 6th April, 1992.

The prosecution's case was that these documents were seditious and so their importation and possession was unlawful. In the High Court, Unyolo, J. agreed with this view. On the first document the court emphasized the following: the observation by Chihana that the pastoral letter reflects the feelings of "millions of Malawians"; what the court called the charge that the authorities "who oppress Malawians ... can only be Godless"; the reference to the Malawi Government as "oppressive and frequently brutal" and as "an island of oppression and corruption". In the document Chihana referred also to the "the long rule of Dr. Banda" whereby "Malawi's human rights have been ruthlessly abused". Chihana said also that the one-party system of government in Malawi had "stifled social and economic progress, individual initiative and creativity" and that the Malawi Congress Party was a party of "darkness and death". So, Chihana called upon all the churches to "speak out and denounce the atrocities of the Malawi Government".

On the second document the court stressed the following: the statement by Chihana that the history of Malawi "shows gross abuse of basic human rights, growing poverty and mass starvation, personalized rule and tyranny by the leadership that brought independence to Malawi"; the summary by Chihana of the history of Malawi as "that of the struggle between the forces of greed and the forces of progres-

19

sive change" and that after 28 years of independence Malawi "still remains the poorest country in the region where mass poverty, starvation, nepotism, tribalism and fanatical mob politics remain the order of the day". The court also emphasized the point that the document refers to "acute income disparity, a growing gap between the rich and poor" and that "the poor are expected to donate their hard–earned tambalas to Dr. Banda and his party" and that "this is 20th century feudalism". In the document Chihana also said that "neither Dr. Banda and his Party ever had a sincere commitment to the interests of the nation"and that that was the reason why "the poor are weeping, but Dr. Banda and his ruling elite are wallowing in luxury"; "they are even prepared to risk the country's economy to ensure their own personal political survival. Is this a responsible Government?" In the document there were also references to the Malawi Congress Party as practicing "rampant intimidation, detention without trial and torture" and "cross–border political assassination".

On the third document the court stressed the statement in it that 6th April, 1992 marked "the beginning of a new era in Malawi", marking "the beginning of the process to organize our peaceful march towards the restoration of basic human rights which have been denied us for the past 30 years". The document listed these human rights as: freedom of speech, freedom to meet and discuss political issues, freedom to belong to a political party of one's choice and the right to elect a government and leaders of one's choice. The court also stressed the complaint in the document that Malawians, including those in the civil service, the police and the Army, had for the past 30 years been victims of "an oppressive system" and that there is "a deep sense of fear, despair and helplessness".

Unyolo, J. found that these documents had a seditious intention because:

> (a) they were characterized by strong words of abuse and contempt; (p. 11) and contained coarse words and scurrilous ridicule on the President and the Government; (p. 11) for example:
>
> (i) the claim that despite the fact that Malawi has been independent for 28 years the country is the poorest in this part of Africa;
>
> (ii) the assertion that mass poverty and starvation are the order of the day in the country; and
>
> (iii) the charge that the President has never had any serious

commitment to the interest of the country. "These are malignant and abusive remarks, in my view". p. 11).

(b) they contained relentless attacks upon the Government, for example:

(i) the Government is described as oppressive, frequently brutal, personalized, tyrannical, Godless, etc.; and

(ii) the assertion that Malawians have for the past 30 years been victims of an oppressive system. "Reading the documents through what comes out is swinging attacks, right through". (p.11); and

(c) they were a catalogue of inflammatory statements and a collocation of defamatory accusations imputing base and dishonourable conduct and practices to the President and the Government. For example, the President is "in pointed language", accused of greed and corruption, such as, that the President and his Party are wallowing in luxury while the poor are weeping and that there exists in Malawi "20th century feudalism where the poor are expected to donate their money to the President."

"Surely, these are both inflammatory and malignant statements". (p.11).

The judge found that, reading the documents as a whole, a seditious intention could be inferred, "namely, an intention to expose the President and the Government to odium and also to excite disaffection against both the President and the Government". (p.11), He dismissed the argument that the documents contained constructive criticism. "It is clear from these statements and sentiments that the accused is full of rancour against both the President and the Government. In my judgement, what we have here cannot be constructive criticism at all". (p.12).

The court held that the statutory defenses in section 50(1), sub section (i) to (iv), were not available to Chihana because:

"what we have here is not, in my judgement, a case where the accused was merely trying to point out errors or defects and saying 'let's put them right'. As I have shown, what we have is a case of mud-throwing and condemnation, all round --- the predominant idea of the writing contained in these documents was to bring the President and the Government into hatred or contempt and also to excite disaffection. Such, in my judgement, was the accused's intention, and I so find". (p. 12).

Unyolo, J. held that the law of Malawi does not require an intention to incite violence as an ingredient of the offence of sedition. He assumed that the Penal Code of Malawi is a Code *strictio sensu* and held that it is clear and unambiguous. On this assumption the absence in the Code of the statement that an intention to incite violence is an ingredient of the offence of sedition amounts to a statement that it is not an ingredient of the offence. He backed himself up with the Gold Coast case of *Wallace–Johnson*, the Northern Rhodesian case of *Buchanan* and the Nyasaland cases of *Chipembere* and *Banda*. He distinguished *Chihana 1992* from the Canadian case of *Boucher* because the Criminal Code of Canada expressly stated that the advocation of force was an ingredient of a seditious intention. He also distinguished *Chihana 1992* from the English case of *Choudhury* because this latter case dealt with the common law rather than the statutory offence of sedition.

On appeal in *Chihana 1993* Banda, C.J. agreed with the lower court and concluded that "the appellant's statements had crossed over the line between political criticism and insult". (p. 9).

I will deal with these points *seriatim* in order to show that it was, in law, easy in *Chihana* to follow *Boucher* and *Choudhury*. The assumption that the Penal Code is a code *stricto sensu* is clearly wrong. The Code itself shows (s.2) that it is not a complete and comprehensive statement of the criminal law. It further states (s.3) that it shall be interpreted in accordance with the principles of legal interpretation in England. The provisions of s. 3 were considered by the Privy Council in the Tanganyika case of *Mawji & Another* where the court said:

> "It may be difficult to define the limits of section [3]. The contrast between substantive law and interpretation does not seem to assist. The most obvious form of interpretation will extend or restrict the application of words and thereby affect the substantive law" (p. 34).

James Read has shown that the only Penal Code in Africa which is a code *stricto sensu* is the Gold Coast Penal Code in force in 1940. (Read, 1963). Unyolo, J. himself read into the Penal Code a statement that "the truth of any seditious material is immaterial so far as guilt is concerned" (p. 15) and supported himself with common law authorities.

Both Unyolo, J. and Banda, C.J. held that the Penal Code is clear and unambiguous. Again this is not so. If the words "contempt, discontent, disaffection, hatred, ill–will, hostility" are given their plain meaning in a criminal statute serious consequences ensue. Any criticism of the President or the Government would be seditious. This would not be consonant with a system of government which feeds on the opinions the Ruled hold of their Rulers. The courts have, therefore, placed some limits on the words used. The Zambian case of *Chitenge* shows that the Penal Code is not clear and unambiguous. There it was held that the word "felony" in the equivalent of s.212(c) does not mean any felony but only such felony as is in itself dangerous to human life. Applied to ss.50 and 51 of the Penal Code the words "contempt, discontent, disaffection, hatred, hostility" mean only those which threaten public safety or public order.

Banda, C.J. also held that it is judicially indefensible to distinguish *Chihana* on the law from *Wallace–Johnson*. For the reasons stated on the first proposition above this proposition is wrong. Furthermore, the failure by Banda, C.J. to take into account the constitutional and political differences between the Gold Coast of 1940 and the Malawi of 1993 is a piece of judicial traditionalism which is difficult to defend. As was shown in *Boucher* whether a court is interpreting a statute or an old judicial decision the time factor is a useful consideration. In that case Locke, J. said that whether the old authorities were to be accepted as binding in 1951 would take into account "*the alteration of the respective functions of the sovereign and the elected representatives of the people since the days preceding the passing of the Bill of Rights in 1688*". (p.395, my emphasis). Even in this country the National Traditional Appeal Court in *Chirwa & Chirwa* refused to have its jurisdiction circumscribed by section 12 of the Traditional Courts Act: "that provision is not good law as it detracts a lot from the powers of a Traditional Court": p.711 of the Court Record.

In the High Court Unyolo, J. held that *Buchanan*, *Chipembere* and *Banda* are binding on the High Court of Malawi and that these decisions had followed *Wallace–Johnson*. *Buchanan* is highly unsatisfactory. Whether the Penal Code is a code *stricto sensu* or not was not discussed. Clayden, F.J. merely said that "the elements of the intention correspond closely to the elements of the intention at common law. --- But as was laid down in *Wallace–Johnson* --- it is in the criminal code --- and not in the English or Scottish cases that the law of sedition for the colony is to be found". (p.525). The judgement in *Banda* was also written and read by Clayden, F.C.J. and is silent on the question of intention. *Chipembere* was also written and read by

Clayden, F.C.J. and there is a statement which supports *Boucher* and *Choudhury*:

> "It seems clear enough --- to this court that the accused, when --- speaking freely about these things by which he is obsessed, would be very likely to utter words which would convey his sense of bitterness against Europeans as a class *and would try to arouse like feelings of anger, hate and violence* which dominate his mind". (p. 89, my emphasis).

On the question of intention the cases of *Buchanan*, *Chipembere* and *Banda* speak with inconclusive and discordant voices, giving the High Court a choice on the interpretation of ss.50 and 51.

Unyolo, J. and Banda, C.J. also held that the case of *Choudhury* is not persuasive in Malawi because it dealt with the common law rather than the statutory offence of sedition. This argument is a repeat of that in *Wallace--Johnson* and Rinfret, C.J.C. who dissented in *Boucher* (p.377). It is that a "Penal Code" is complete in itself and it is illegitimate to look outside it. It has been shown (Read, 1963) that English--speaking African criminal laws fall into four groups: Sierra Leone which does not have a Penal Code; the Sudan, the Northern Region of the Somali Republic and the Northern Region of Nigeria; the rest of Nigeria, Gambia, Kenya, Malawi, Zambia, Zanzibar, and Uganda; and finally, Ghana. Read states: "Ghana's Criminal Code --- is unique in Africa". (p.5). It is unfortunate that *Wallace--Johnson* which was decided on the Code which is unique in Africa and has a provision to the opposite effect of the Penal Codes in the Malawi group should be used as a guide in interpreting the Malawi group of Penal Codes. *Chitenge* sets out to reverse this practice and there is no good reason in law why *Chihana 1993* refused to follow Chitenge on this point.

Unyolo, J. and Banda, C.J. also refused to follow *Boucher* because, they said, in that case s.133 (4) of the Criminal Code of Canada included force in the definition of seditious intention as follows:

> "Without limiting the generality of the meaning of the expression 'seditious intention', everyone shall be presumed to have a seditious intention who publishes --- any document in which it is advocated --- the use, without the authority of law, of force, as a means of accomplishing any governmental change within Canada".

24

Six out of nine judges insisted that an intention to incite violence was an ingredient of the offence of sedition. After referring to s. 133(4) Kellock, J. said (p. 380):

> "So far as the Code is concerned 'seditious intention' is not defined apart from this sub-section --- *and one is forced back to the common law*. The pamphlet here in question does not, of course, come within the said sub-section". (My emphasis).

Similarly, notwithstanding the opening words of s.133(4) Estey, J. said (p. 393):

> "With great respect, I am of the opinion that *in all cases* the intention to incite violence or public disorder or unlawful conduct against His Majesty or an institution of the state is essential." (My emphasis).

Even Cartwright, J. who otherwise dissented with the minority, agreed with Kellock, J. and said (p. 409):

> "[B]efore a writing can be held to disclose a seditious intention by reason of being calculated to promote feelings of ill-will and hostility between different classes of His Majesty's subjects *it must further appear that the intended or natural and probable, consequence of such promotion of ill-will and hostility is to produce disturbance of or resistance to the authority of lawfully constituted Government*". (My emphasis).

It is, therefore, not easy to distinguish *Chihana* from *Boucher* on the basis of s.133(4) of the Criminal Code of Canada. As stated in *Choudhury* "the common law of sedition or seditious libel was accurately stated in --- *Boucher*". (1 All E.R. at 322).

4. Sedition in the Better Malawi

Both Unyolo, J. and Banda, C.J. dealt with the statutory defences in one short paragraph. In so doing they both failed to transplant the law of sedition from a monarchical system of government to a republican system of government. In the latter system of government all speaking and writing by the second group of citizens is intended to show that the rulers, the first group of citizens, are or have become so unfit to rule that they should constitutionally be replaced by other rulers. In the course of doing this, unintended contempt, disaffection, discontent, hatred, hostility or ill–will may be brought, excited, promoted or raised against the President or the government. This is the crux of the statutory defences. These defences should, therefore, be interpreted as follows:

It is not a seditious intention

(i) to show that the President has been misled or mistaken in any of his measures even though in the course of doing so you bring him or his Government into hatred or contempt or excite disaffection against him or the Government;

(ii) to point out errors or defects in the Government or Constitution or in legislation or in the administration of justice with a view to the remedying of such errors or defects even though in the course of doing so you bring the Government into hatred or contempt or you excite disaffection against the administration of justice in the Republic;

(iii) to persuade the subjects of the President to attempt to procure by lawful means the alteration of any matter in the Republic even though in the course of doing so you excite the subjects of the President to procure the alteration, otherwise than by lawful means, of any other matter in the Republic;

(iv) to point out with a view to their removal, any matters which are producing or have a tendency to produce feelings of ill–will and enmity between different classes of the population of the Republic even though in the course of doing so you promote feelings of ill– will and hostility between different classes of the population of the Republic; and

(v) to do (i) or (ii) or (iii) or (iv) above even though in the course of doing so you raise discontent or disaffection among the subjects of the President.

When section 50(1) is arranged as suggested there is an apparent contradiction within its various paragraphs. In order to resolve this contradiction one needs to realize that these statutory defences work in a manner similar to the defence of self–defence on a charge of murder. There the defence is not that the accused did not kill the victim nor that the accused killed the victim without the necessary intention. The defence is that the accused killed the victim in order to prevent the victim from killing the accused or someone else related to the accused: *Zabroni* and *Jackson*. In a republican system of government attempts to persuade citizens to vote against current Rulers are intended to show that those Rulers are unsuitable for office. And this will most likely, if not necessarily, bring those Rulers into hatred or contempt or raise discontent or disaffection amongst the citizens. If these words ––– contempt, disaffection, discontent, hatred, hostility or ill–will ––– are interpreted literally then the law of sedition necessarily works against republican democracy and is necessarily unconstitutional. In *Chihana 1993* the defence urged the court to redeem the law of sedition from this deep end. In his reply Banda, C.J., on the authority of section 2(1)(iii) of the Constitution, accepted "that the UNO Universal Declaration of Human Rights is part of the law of Malawi and that the freedoms which that Declaration guarantees must be respected and can be enforced in these courts" (p. 2)

> "It seems to us, therefore, that it is the right of every citizen of the Republic of Malawi to have a candid, full and free discussion on any matter of public interest. It is open to every citizen of the Republic to express his or her concern on any aspect of Government policy. This court must be the protector of the fundamental Human Rights which are part of our law." (p. 2).

The Chief Justice further held that "that right to freedom of speech or expression may be subject to restrictions and limitations". Whether a law of sedition is inconsistent with a constitution which guarantees the right of freedom of speech and expression:

> "must and will depend upon the facts and circumstances of each particular case having regard to the words of a particular law of sedition and the provisions of the Constitution in issue". (p. 3 per Banda, C.J.).

Having laid down this as the test the Court should have interpreted the law of sedition, sections 50 and 51 of the Penal Code, in order to see whether it is

> "reasonably required in the interests of defence, public safety, public order or the national economy." (Constitution, s.2(2)).

Nowhere in the judgement does Banda, C.J. discuss and analyse the concepts of defence, public safety, public order or the national economy. Had he done this he would have held that the only ingredient which resolves the apparent inconsistency between sections 50 and 51 of the Penal Code on the one hand and the Constitution on the other is that of an intention to incite violence. The common law has added this further ingredient to the crime of sedition: that the intention is not seditious unless it is an intention to incite violence. This is the law of Canada and of England. In this paper I hope I have shown that this has been the law of Malawi even before it was changed in 1993 by Parliament to follow the rest of the Commonwealth.

5. Conclusion

The story leading to Independence is familiar. As the wind of change blew stronger more Malawians joined the struggle: many suffered in the process; some even lost their lives. This led to the constitutional talks in London which were a re-negotiation of the terms of the social contract so that Africans get the right to take part in the government of their country and get out of the Federation. The use of the criminal law to prevent or delay this struggle failed and Africans got what they were fighting for.

There is sufficient evidence in the documents considered by Unyolo, J. in *Chihana 1992* to show that whatever the contempt, disaffection, discontent, hatred, hostility or ill-will they brought, excited, promoted or raised against the President or the Government the intention was to further the cause of democracy. This was to be done by persuading a sufficient number of those citizens of Malawi who were or appeared to be indifferent to the terms of the social contract as altered or interpreted by the Rulers between 1964 and 1991 to join the struggle for change. These terms included the following. Freedom of association in the political field which had been abolished in 1966 by the introduction of a one-party system of government. This has been regained. The Bill of Rights was excluded from the Constitution in 1966 and there followed gross abuse of human rights between 1966 and 1991. (Machika, 1984). The Bill of Rights has also been re-introduced. Presidential elections were abolished in 1970 during the life of Dr. Kamuzu Banda by providing for his life presidency in the 1966 Constitution. This is now repealed. Parliamentary elections had their meaning reduced by the practice of presidential vetting of parliamentary candidates and by the President's power to nominate an unspecified number of Members of Parliament. This will no longer be the case. And slave-like practices were introduced in the form of the tenancy system of agriculture. This will have to be stopped or continued depending on which political party forms the Government in May, 1994. These gains in the terms of the social contract have been made in the face of a government which has used the criminal law to attempt to prevent or delay political change. The use of the criminal law has caused a lot of suffering but it has also helped many to join the struggle for change.

Bibliography

I. Legislation:

A. Malawi Independence Order, 1964
B. Independence Constitution 1964
C. Malawi Constitution 1966
D. Penal Code (Cap 7:01, Laws of Malawi) ss.2, 3, 50, 51, 212(c)

II. Judicial decisions:

A. Nyasaland/Malawi:

1. *Attorney–General* v. *Jackson* (1956) 1 ALR Mal. 488.
2. *Banda* v. R. (1961) 2 ALR. Mal. 111.
3. *Chihana* v. *Rep.*, M.S.C.A. Crim. App. No. 9 of 1992 (Banda, C.J.;
   Mkandawire and Mbalame, J.J.A.).
4. *Chipembere* v. *R.* (1961) 2 ALR Mal. 83.
5. *Chirwa & Chirwa* v. *The Republic*, Crim. App. Case No. 5 of 1983
   (N.T.A.C., 1984) (Unreported).
6. *Rep* v. *Chihana*, Crim. Case No. 1 of 1992 (HC) (Unyolo, J.)
7. *Zabroni* v. *R.* (1956) 1 ALR. Mal. 353.

B. Comparative:

1. Canada:
   Boucher v. *The King* [1951] 2 D.L.R. 369

2. England:
   R. v. *Chief Metropolitan Stipendiary Magistrate, Ex p. Choudhury*
   [1991] 1 Q.B. 429, [1991] 1 All E.R. 306.

3. Gold Coast/Ghana:
   Wallace–Johnson v. *The King* [1940] A.C. 231.

4. Northern Rhodesia/Zambia:
   a. *Buchanan* v. *R* (1957) R & N. 523.
   b. *Chitenge* v. *The People* [1966] ZR. 37.

5. Tanganyika/Tanzania:
   Mawji & Another v. *The Queen* [1957] A.C. 126.

III. Books:

Dahrendorf, Ralph, *Law and Order* (London: Stevens, 1985).

IV. Articles:

Machika, M.R.E. "The Law and Liberty of Movement Revisited" (Chancellor College, Zomba: Staff Seminar Paper No. 43, 1984).
Read, James "Criminal Law in the Africa of Today and Tomorrow" [1963] J.A.L. 5.

3. Not Catalyst But Ferment: The Distinctive Contribution of the Churches to Political Reform in Malawi 1992–93

Kenneth R. Ross

1. Introduction

Hans Küng has recently written that, contrary to the expectations of generations of Marxist philosophers, "from Eastern Europe and East Germany through South Africa to South America and the Philippines it has proved that religion can be not only a means of social appeasement and consolation but also ... a catalyst of social liberation: and this without that revolutionary use of force which results in a vicious circle of ever–new violence."[1] The (relatively) peaceful overthrow of the one–party system in Malawi has been no exception. When it was announced that the majority had voted for multi–party government in the national referendum on political pluralism held on 14 June 1993, jubilant crowds in the urban centres marched first to the Bishop's House. This was their immediate acknowledgement that they owed their new found freedom to the Catholic bishops who had been the first to openly challenge the one–party system.[2] They were recalling

---

[1] H. Küng, *Credo: The Apostles' Creed Explained for Today*, (London: SCM, 1992), p. 13.

[2] For the imposition of one–party rule in Malawi see P. Short, *Banda*, (London and Boston: Routledge and Kegan Paul, 1974); T.D. Williams, *Malawi: The Politics of Despair*, (Ithaca and London: Cornell University Press, 1978); and J.L. Lwanda, *Kamuzu Banda of Malawi: A Study in Promise, Power and Paralysis*, (Glasgow: Dudu Nsomba Publications, 1993). For the denial of human rights and the totalitarian nature of MCP rule see *Where Silence Rules: The Suppression of Dissent in Malawi*, (Washington and London: Africa Watch, 1990); *Malawi: Human Rights Violations 25 Years After Independence*, (London: Amnesty International, 1989); *Malawi: Prison Conditions, Cruel Punishment and Detention Without Trial*, (London: Amnesty International, 1992); *Human Rights in Malawi*, (London: Law Society of England and Wales, 1992); *Malawi: Preserving the One–Party State*, London: Amnesty International, 1993); and *The Referendum in Malawi: Free Expression Denied*, (London: Article 19, Issue 22, April 1993). For an overview of

the Pastoral Letter issued by the Bishops at Lent 1992, a document of such importance that, in common parlance, modern Malawian history is divided between "before the Pastoral Letter" and "since the Pastoral Letter"! The Bishops' statement was the first public criticism of the Malawi Congress Party regime to be issued in the country since independence in 1964 and called for far-reaching social and political reform.[3] The government moved swiftly to ban the Letter and for a time there were fears for the lives of the Bishops. Soon, however, student marches and workers' strikes, unprecedented in Malawi, demonstrated popular support for the Bishops' initiative. When donor countries agreed in May to suspend development aid until there was an improvement in Malawi's record on issues of governance and human rights, it was clear that the one-party system was facing its most serious crisis.

The Presbyterian Church took up the initiative in June with a call for the appointment of a broadly based Commission charged with responsibility for the reform of the political system.[4] By October the "Public Affairs Committee" had been formed in response to this call. The PAC brought together religious leaders, the emerging opposition politicians and representatives of commerce, industry and the legal profession. It became, to a significant extent, the engine of the process of political reform. Their high profile in the reform movement exposed the church leaders to considerable danger in a country where any hint of opposition had been ruthlessly and often violently elimi-nated. Mgr. John Roche, who was held to be responsible for drafting the Pastoral Letter, was expelled from Malawi on 17 April 1992. Rev Aaron Longwe, the Presbyterian minister most forthright in taking up the social and political issues, was repeatedly detained. Many church

---

modern Malawian history, including the events of 1992–93 see *Malawi: A Moment of Truth*, (London: Catholic Institute for International Relations, July 1993); and *Kirche und Gesellschaft in Malawi: Die Krise von 1992 in historischer Perspektive*, (Hamburg: EMW Informationen No. 98, February 1993).

[3] The Pastoral Letter was published in March 1992 in Malawi under the title *Living Our Faith*; in September 1992 it was published under the title *The Truth Will Set You Free* (Church in the World No. 28) by the Catholic Institute of International Relations in London.

[4] See "The Nation of Malawi in Crisis: the Church's Concern", Geneva: World Alliance of Reformed Churches, 2 June 1992, p. 2.

leaders were harassed and received death threats.[5] It was at very considerable personal cost that they spearheaded the confrontation of the people with the government. Their witness bore fruit, however, in the peaceful transition to multi-party democracy signalled by the defeat of the Malawi Congress Party in the national referendum. The purpose of this paper is to identify some of the factors which operated to make the churches effective as agents of social liberation in the Malawi context.

2. The Preferential Option for the Poor

One of the most powerful movements within the Christian faith over the last twenty-five years has been that which stresses the calling of the church to identify with the poor and oppressed. Approaches vary from the revolutionary to the paternalistic but the consensus is inescapable: the church is called to solidarity with the poor, the dispossessed, the exploited, the marginalized. This solidarity has led the church to understand that, as Miguez Bonino has written, "the poor are not morally or spiritually superior to others, but they do see reality from a different angle or location – and therefore differently."[6] This is the angle or location from which the church is mandated to approach social and political realities. Such a radical orientation to the dispossessed and disadvantaged sections of society cannot fail to operate as a powerful political dynamic in the drive for social justice. It unashamedly seeks to inject bias into the political process, i.e. that it should be biased in favour of the poor. It commits the church to seeking the political empowerment of the masses of ordinary people who tend to be excluded and exploited. The Pastoral Letter of Lent 1992 was written from this perspective of a preferential option for the poor. Its social critique opens with these words: "In our society we are aware of a growing gap between the rich and the poor with regard to

---

5 A particularly notorious incident occurred in November 1992 when Rev Misanjo Kansilanga, Senior Clerk to the General Synod of the Church of Central Africa Presbyterian, was issued with a death threat by an MCP chairman at a public meeting at which President Banda was present. See Letter from the CCAP Synod of Blantyre to the Hon. J.Z.U. Tembo, Minister of State, on "Public Denunciation of the Rev Misanjo E. Kansilanga", 6 November 1992.
6 J. Miguez Bonino, *Toward a Christian Political Ethics*, (Philadelphia: Fortress Press, 1983), p. 43.

expectations, living standards and development. Many people still live in circumstances which are hardly compatible with their dignity as sons and daughters of God. Their life is a struggle for survival. At the same time a minority enjoys the fruits of development and can afford to live in luxury and wealth. We appeal for a more just distribution of the nation's wealth."[7] It was from this perspective and on this basis that the Bishops challenged the status quo on such issues as wage structure, education and health services, human rights and democratic accountability of government.

Likewise the follow-up Presbyterian statement called for the appointment of a Commission not only to reform the political system but "to look into the distribution of income and wealth required by the demands of social justice."[8] The identification of the church with the plight of the poor was an important factor in enabling its leaders to mount a radical challenge to the prevailing political system. When questioned about the origins of the Pastoral Letter, one of the Bishops replied, "I did not write the Letter; it was written a long time ago on the hearts of our people."[9] Much of the Letter must be read as an echo of what Malawian Catholics have been saying to their priests over the years. This helps to account for the extraordinary width of support which the Letter immediately provoked. The churches were in touch with the people and able to be the voice of the poor. Day to day experience in the parishes gave the church leaders an understanding of the real facts of life in Malawi and an ability to see things from the standpoint of the poor – something which eluded those confined to the rarified atmosphere of the corridors of power. At a time of crisis this gave the churches a position of quite decisive political importance. At the same time, the preferential option for the poor brought a radical challenge to the churches themselves since they had tended too much to mirror the very structures of domination and oppression which they were criticizing in the political system. Judgement begins with the house of God!

---

7 *Living Our Faith*, p. 2.
8 "The Nation of Malawi in Crisis: the Church's Concern", p. 2.
9 Unattributable interview.

3. The International Character of the Church

The churches were also equipped to play a distinctive role in facilitating the social transition in Malawi by their relationships within the worldwide church. A sense of belonging and accountability within a wider community of faith gave the churches a certain independence within the highly totalitarian social and political structures prevailing in Malawi. In their preparation of the epochal Pastoral Letter the Catholic Bishops were deeply influenced by the theology and witness of the church worldwide. Since Vatican II the Catholic Church has demonstrated an increased appreciation that Christian faith demands solidarity with the poor and disadvantaged. Mgr John Roche claimed that this cultivated a readiness to speak out against exploitation and oppression and promoted "a growing awareness amongst the Christian community in Malawi that human rights are part of the Gospel".[10] The Bishops themselves were impressed by the courageous prophetic witness of Episcopal Conferences in other African countries such as Kenya and Zimbabwe. They also remembered that, during the Pope's visit to Malawi in 1989, "he did not say anything in public concerning human rights but did so to the Bishops and stated that it was an integral part of the Gospel especially where there was lack of such rights."[11] The Pastoral Letter owed no small part of its inspiration to the strong international links and contacts which characterize the Roman Catholic Church. On the Presbyterian side, the role of the World Alliance of Reformed Churches, especially through the visit of their delegation in June 1992, in offering solidarity and practical support was of great value in enabling the Malawian leaders to take the effective stand which they did. This international solidarity made it much more difficult for the government to take action against church leaders whom it considered troublesome and certainly was a contributory factor in the speedy release of most of those who were arrested. The sensitivity of the government to these international links was demonstrated when members of the Public Affairs Committee went to England to confer with the Council of Churches in Britain and Ireland from 17 to 19 February 1993. The Malawi government insisted that its own ministerial delegation should attend the meeting

---

10 Mgr John Roche, Apostolic Administrator of the Diocese of Mzuzu, Press Conference, London, 12 May 1992.
11 *Ibid.*

to present its case and was humiliated and infuriated when the delegation was turned away from the church conference which condemned government resistance to democratic change.[12] The catholic character of the church, when given such practical expression, served to heighten its moral authority within the political arena. At the same time, the expectations of partners overseas that the church should struggle for social justice at a time of crisis, had a galvanising effect on the churches in Malawi.

4. The Dangerous Memory

In addition to their relations to the poor in Malawi and to the world-wide church, the churches had another quite distinctive reference point. This was their scriptures and tradition of worship. These proved to be the sources from which a renewed social witness was developed. Many, many sermons sought to relate biblical teaching directly to social and political affairs in Malawi. This contributed significantly to the grassroots awareness that the country was in need of radical political change and helped to produce the faith and the hope that this could be achieved. Johan–Baptist Metz has written of the "dangerous memory" or "subversive memory" of Jesus Christ which the church carries through history. Time and again "this definite memory breaks through the magic circle of the prevailing consciousness."[13] Where an unjust and oppressive system of government is established and held in place by tight control and powerful propaganda it is possible to develop such a culture of deceit that people lose their bearings and even their thinking is "colonized" by the "system". The Christian proclamation is one force which can break through that false consciousness by making the system accountable to the norms and values of the kingdom of God. The Malawi case supplies rather a dramatic instance. From the Cabinet Crisis of 1964 the Malawi Congress Party succeeded by ceaseless propaganda in creating a culture of deceit which seemed impregnable until the Pastoral Letter of 1992 broke through the "magic circle" in which the people were trapped.[14]

---

12 *Daily Times*, 4 March 1993.

13 J.B. Metz, *Faith in History and Society: Toward a Practical Fundamental Theology*, (London: Burns & Oates, 1980), pp. 89–90.

14 The Cabinet Crisis broke only a few weeks after independence in 1964 and marked the defeat of the ministers who favoured "open" government and the

Thereafter the MCP government could no longer be "a law unto itself" for the church was measuring the policies and actions of the government against the norm or criterion of the biblical message of the kingdom of God. By weighing the existing order against the demands of God's impending kingdom the church supplied a gauge which freed people to make their own assessment of the prevailing system and to take action accordingly. The church's memory did prove to be "dangerous" and "subversive" so far as the political system in Malawi was concerned. The savagery with which the MCP turned on the Catholic Bishops was testimony to that.[15]

5. Political Order and Religious Legitimation

Philip Wogaman recently observed that, "any political philosophy remains incomplete unless it has reference to a vision of what is ultimately true and ultimately good, and that is the contribution of theological traditions."[16] Politics needs religion. Even Machiavelli realised that the ruler must *seem* to be moral and religious! The MCP government in Malawi was well aware of the power of religion in the political realm. Systematically and successfully it pressed the churches into service to supply it with religious legitimation. Much publicity was given to the Life President's occasional appearances in church, visits of international church leaders were treated as state occasions, national worship services were held regularly and it was mandatory at any church service to give thanks and pray for the Life President. The way in which the MCP political system was upheld by such religious

---

beginning of the totalitarian one-party system. No one who lived through the time of the issue of the Pastoral Letter will be able to forget the experience. It was like the moment in the fairy-tale when the little boy pointed out that the Emperor had no clothes! Things could never be the same again. Practically overnight the mode of discourse in everyday conversation changed. One moment the MCP was all-powerful; the next it was becoming a scandal and a laughing stock. The sense of liberation was palpable. Of course, there were a number of forces bringing about this revolution in consciousness but the Pastoral Letter, by common consent, was the turning point.

[15] Records of the MCP Emergency Convention at which a plan to kill the Bishops was discussed have been circulated widely both inside and outside Malawi. See, e.g., *The Nation*, Vol. 1 Nos. 12-21 (2 Sept.-4 Oct. 1993).

[16] J.P. Wogaman, Christian Perspectives on Politics, (London: SCM, 1988), p. 110.

legitimation was recognised in the statement issued by the Blantyre Synod of the CCAP in January 1993: "Because of this very verbal stance on the side of the MCP (during the independence struggle), after Independence, the CCAP was aligned closely with the government and became so assimilated with the government's activities that the Synod was often invited to pray and participate as a Church at various government functions. However, because of this assimilation and alignment with the MCP, the Church gradually lost its ability to admonish or speak pastorally to the government. We do not want to make the same mistake at this time in order to ensure that the Church retains its prophetic voice throughout the coming years of our country's history."[17] When the raising of the prophetic voice led to government cries that "the church is meddling in politics!" what it actually wanted was for the church to continue supplying unquestioning legitimation of the status quo rather than raising awkward questions of justice!

The importance which the MCP attached to religious legitimation can be measured by the extent to which it was stung by the Pastoral Letter into serious over-reaction.[18] It is further indicated by the importance which the government attached to the continuing support of the CCAP Nkhoma Synod after all other "mainline" churches had withdrawn their legitimation. As it struggled to retain an air of legitimacy it turned to ministers of the Nkhoma Synod to officiate at government functions and to generally show solidarity with the MCP. This they were willing to do and were rewarded accordingly with government patronage. Finally, however, when even Nkhoma Synod's support became lukewarm, the MCP was forced to supply its own religious legitimation. When it launched its campaign newspaper, the *Guardian Today*, it was striking to note how many articles were devoted to portraying the MCP as having a divine mandate. This was epitomized by a cartoon series on the theme "MCP Points to God!; Multi-Party – Horns of the Devil!"[19] Such desperate propaganda revealed how much the MCP government had depended on the legitimation which it had received from the churches during the preceding years. Once the

---

[17] "A Statement on the Role of the Church in the Transformation of Malawi in the Context of Justice and Peace", Produced by the Administrators Conference, Blantyre Synod CCAP, January 22–23, 1993, p.4.

[18] See, e.g., editorial entitled "No Mercy" in *Malawi News*, 14–20 March 1992.

[19] See, e.g., *Guardian Today*, Vol. 1, No. 7, May 19–25 1993.

churches had broken out of that idelogical captivity, the MCP government faced a crisis of legitimacy which it was unable to surmount. On the other hand, the emergent opposition was able constantly to appeal to the prophetic critique of the churches as justification for its political initiative.[20] It was no surprise that, when UDF leader Bakili Muluzi made his victory speech after the national referendum, he went out of his way to thank the churches: "In particular, I would like to single out the seven Catholic Bishops and the [Presbyterian] Blantyre Synod."[21] In a country where the Christian faith is highly esteemed by a large proportion of the population, the legitimacy which the churches bestowed on the opposition movement, in face of government attempts to brand its leaders "dissidents" and "confusionists", was a considerable factor in enabling the forces of change to succeed.

6. Church Unity and Diversity

Christianity in Malawi is by no means organised as a monolithic institution. There are many churches, each with its own distinctive tradition. Of particular significance in the transition of 1992–93 were the distinctive styles of social engagement found in the Roman Catholic and Presbyterian churches. As Ernst Troeltsch observed, Catholicism tends to express its social responsibility "in particular institutions and occasional interventions in affairs."[22] The Pastoral Letter as such an "intervention", perhaps one of the most brilliant and decisive, but after its issue the Bishops stepped back until they judged that another "intervention" was called for.[23] Troeltsch observed that the Presbyterian or Reformed tradition, by contrast, is marked by "a systematic endeavour to mould the life of society as a whole ... it lays down the principle that the church ought to be interested in all sides of

---

20 This was evident in the speech made by Mr Chakufwa Chihana , before he was arrested on the airport tarmac when he returned to Malawi in April 1992 to lead a pro-democracy movement, during which he appealed to the Catholic Bishops' Pastoral Letter. *Independent* (British newspaper), 8 April 1992.

21 *UDF News*, Vol. 1 No. 21, 17–24 June 1993.

22 E. Troeltsch, *The Social Teaching of the Christian Churches*, Vol. 2, (New York: Macmillan, 1931), p. 602.

23 In February 1993 they issued a further Pastoral Letter entitled "Choosing our Future", which specifically addressed the upcoming national referendum.

life."[24] It was the Presbyterians, in the crisis provoked by the Pastoral Letter, who took direct responsibility for the political process, particularly through the formation of the Public Affairs Committee.[25] This body was the most effective agent in putting into effect the social and political changes for which the Bishops had called. The two approaches proved to be significantly complementary. It was the prophetic voice of the Catholic Bishops which awakened the nation to the need for radical social change. It was the "hands-on" engagement of the Presbyterians which translated the awakening into a coherent and well-organised movement for political reform. At the same time, the unity of the churches was no less important than their diversity in approach. When the Pastoral Letter was issued the government sought to provoke a rift between the churches. President Banda, as a Presbyterian himself, alleged that the Letter had been written because Catholics hated Presbyterians. It was enormously important that the Presbyterians resisted the pressure to rally behind the government and stood firm instead with the Bishops.[26] With the exception of the Nkhoma Synod and a few renegade Catholic priests, the government was not able to penetrate the churches' united front which was further consolidated in late 1992 and early 1993 when the PAC and the Christian Council of Malawi emerged as formidable forces on the political scene. Indeed, having stood together through the crisis it appears that the churches in Malawi are more united today than for many years. This may prove to have further political significance as the nation faces the spectre of regionalism and tribalism. The challenge then to the church is how far it is captive to such forces and how far it is able to transcend them through unity in the faith. While that challenge already provoked a struggle in 1992-93, we can recognise that both the diversity and the unity of the churches contributed importantly to the social transition in Malawi.

---

[24] Troeltsch, *ibid* , p. 602.

[25] The Presbyterians brought together representatives of the CCAP, the Roman Catholic and Anglican churches, the Muslim community, the Malawi Law Society, and the Associated Chambers of Commerce and Industry in Malawi. When the government met with the PAC on 19 October 1992 it was the first time a non-party organisation had been acknowledged as having a part to play in national political affairs.

[26] This solidarity was strongly expressed, e.g., by Rev Dr Chris Wigglesworth, General Secretary of the Church of Scotland Board of World Mission and Unity, in a BBC broadcast aired on 13 March 1992.

7. Not Catalyst But Ferment

A fair appraisal of church life in the social crisis has to take account not only of unity and diversity but also serious division. This was found most markedly in the Presbyterian Church where, as we have noted, the Nkhoma Synod, which originated in a Mission of the Dutch Reformed Church of Cape Province, South Africa, took a position directly opposed to the Scottish–originated Blantyre and Livingstonia Synods.[27] Nkhoma support for the government may be accounted for both by the ethos of the DRC and its location in the Central Region – the political power base of President Banda and the inner circle of the MCP who have personal historical links with the Synod. Nevertheless, the other churches were dismayed when a Nkhoma Synod minister disowned, having originally signed, a Christian Council letter which was critical of the government on issues of human rights and governance and called for a national referendum on the one–party system. The Christian Council responded by voting to suspend Nkhoma Synod from membership of the Council.[28] At a time when church leaders were making a risky and costly prophetic social witness, the other churches felt betrayed that Nkhoma Synod appeared to be lining up against them in the struggle for justice and truth in Malawi. This was a painful experience for the churches and the wounds may take long to heal. However, the very intensity of the struggle within the life of the churches may also be understood as a distinctive contribution to the national transition. John de Gruchy has recently written that "the struggle for liberation, justice and truth in the world is not simply a struggle *between* the church and the powers of the world beyond its boundaries, but a struggle *within the life of the church itself* – a struggle for the soul of the church that relates to the social struggles of the world. This is not clearly recognised in times of relative harmony and peace ... but *in times of social and political crisis it becomes intensely apparent*."[29]

---

[27] For the origins of Nkhoma Synod see C.M. Pauw, "Mission and Church in Malawi: The History of the Nkhoma Synod of the Church of Central Africa, Presbyterian 1889–1962", D.Th., University of Stellenbosch, 1980.

[28] Open Letter to the Government of Malawi, from the Christian Council of Malawi, 26 August 1992; Daily Times, 6 November 1992.

[29] J.W. de Gruchy, *Liberating Reformed Theology: A South African Contribution to an Ecumenical Debate*, (Grand Rapids: Eerdmans & Cape Town:

Such times came to Malawi in 1992–93. The battle was waged not only *between* the churches and the repressive political system but *within* and *among* the churches themselves. The struggle for the soul of the church was evident in, e.g., Blantyre Synod's statement of repentance for its ideological captivity or Nkhoma Synod's failure to perceive and rise to the ethical demands of the gospel in the contemporary situation. It is evident in the personal *kairos* which came to many individual Christians as they sought to respond with integrity to the social crisis and stood out at great risk and at great cost. The division and the struggle within the life of the church suggest that it was not *catalyst* but *ferment*, to borrow the term which de Gruchy employs to describe the church's social engagement.[30] Hans Küng's word *catalyst* suggests that the agent of social change is itself constant and unchanged throughout the process. *Ferment* much more adequately describes the condition of the churches in Malawi in 1992–93 as they responded to their identification with the poor, capitalized on their relations within the worldwide church, recalled the "dangerous memory" of Jesus Christ, assessed and adjusted the religious legitimation which they offered, marshalled the resources both of their diversity and of their unity, and came to terms with painful struggles and divisions. It was a ferment through which the churches were chastened, challenged, changed and matured. It was a crisis of judgement and repentance – which, when it was released into the national life through the church's witness, proved to be a ferment of transformation powerful to contribute to the making of a new Malawi.

David Philip, 1991), p. 220, my italics.
[30] *Ibid*, pp. 1–46 *et passim*. So far as I know, the image of the Christian faith working as a "ferment in history" first gained currency in Latin American Liberation Theology but it is particularly well developed in de Gruchy's *Liberating Reformed Theology*.

4. 'A Raging Calm'? – The Impact of Labour Relations on Politics in Malawi

Gracian Zibelu Banda

1. Introduction: Labour, Unionism and the Law

The enormity of the problem faced by those concerned with protection of workers' rights has been accentuated in recent years both in Industrialised Countries (ICs) and Less Developed Countries (LDCs) not least by the world economic crisis.[1] A high rate of unemployment has thrown organised labour off balance to the extent where it is becoming increasingly difficult to defend its members' job security. The 'new' international division of labour which certain theorists announced in the latter part of the 1980s, under which LDCs would gain from a relocation of industries from ICs, provided a new gleam of hope for impoverished LDCs. Such hopes have not only been largely unfulfilled but where there has been any tangible results at all repression of labour rights has been on the ascendance (Southal, 1989; Adelman, 1990; Wangel, 1988).

For the great majority of LDCs where the bulk of the population barely ekes out a living from subsistence agriculture there is little hope that LDCs' labour can effectively organise to a level which would impact the protection of workers' rights. The International Labour Organisation (ILO), which is the major organisation concerned with protection of workers' rights, finds itself increasingly weakened in the face of the dosage of economic doctrines of the more influential financial institutions – the World Bank and the International Monetary Fund (IMF).[2] These institutions extend credits to

---

[1] Add to this the advent of anti-labour attitudes of the free market governments of Reagan and Thatcher in the 1980s. There was little impetus for protecting workers' rights.

[2] A number of other factors account for the ILO's inefficiency. The tripartite nature of the organisation demands that states, workers and employers find a more or less common ground in articulating conventions. The machinery of enforcement is not as efficient (Adelman, 1989).

LDCs on conditionalities which necessarily entail impinging not only on workers' economic rights but on fundamental human rights as a whole.

The free market principles in vogue from these financial institutions appear to be supported by the common law. Under the doctrine of 'freedom of contract' the law assumes legal actors who enter into contracts as free agents and that therefore they should not be constrained by law when entering into the contract. This doctrine applies to employment contracts with equal force even though it is abundantly clear that the economic might of the employer substantially puts the employee at a disadvantaged bargaining position. That such freedom of contract simply provides an opportunity for the powerful to dictate terms to the weak (Berenson & Benedictus, 1987) is conveniently ignored on the basis of free markets. Thus from very early times the common law consistently whittled down attempts by workers to organise for the sake of negotiating with the employer to the extent that it had to take a Government losing elections in England in the nineteenth century for Parliament to pass legislation legalising trade unions (Kahn-Freund, 1972). The law consistently took its traditional view of ignoring social reality.[3]

Partly as a result of the conditions in which the law evolved and partly as a result of a kind of theorising which barely looks ahead of one's nose common lawyers and industrial relations theorists delimit the province of labour law as applying to industrial (mainly factory) workers and those in the mainstream economy. A whole fabric of society that does not depend on a wage or salary is ignored or conveniently side-lined, left in 'pending' trays until they 'graduate' into the mainstream economy. Thus subsistence farmers, share croppers, small scale traders, street vendors are not recognised workers, hence outside the ambit of labour law.

The argument in this paper is that the law and economic policy mostly derived from ICs ignore and in most respects suppress the largest proportion of workers in LDCs, including Malawi. A look at labour

---

[3] It is said that the common law does not recognise any disequilibrium of power arising from normal social relations such as economic power as distinct from abnormal personal conditions such as infancy (Kahn-Freund, 1972:26). This hardly explains or justifies the law's attitude because it begs questions such as: how did the 'normal' condition arise? Is it indeed normal?

legislation in Malawi appears to suggest that the law has had difficulties jettisoning the 'freedom of contract' concept and appears to cling to it while at the same time allowing the state to take a very active role in regulating labour. The state has used its political and economic muscle to suppress genuine participation of workers in decision making in economic activity. In the process the state antagonised itself to workers from all sectors of the economy. Although labour did not protest overtly as was happening in other countries more subtle means of resistance were visible. The events which unfolded in 1992 and 1993 relating to worker activism may be seen as a spontaneous reaction of a labour that has long been denied a grievance mechanism through which issues could have been resolved. These workers see the ruling elite as major obstacle to the betterment of their standards of living. Labour activism is thus not confined to economic unionism. It is a politically engaged labour as well.

2. Trade Unions and the Law

The form labour law has taken under the common law has as much to do with common law tradition as it has with the industrial relations school of thought. The world of the industrial relations school of thought is "... a formal, carefully constructed, but often ahistorical world. Therein is found a tight bargaining environment where collective agreements, grievances handling, arbitration and conciliation procedures, contracts and negotiations take place". Labour in this scheme of things is allowed to form trade unions which are "institutionally protected but legally regulated and constrained" (Cohen, 1987:4)

This is the world envisaged by the Trade Unions Act[4] and the Trade Disputes (Arbitration and Settlement) Act[5]. The Trade Unions Act appears to assume that trade unions would, apart from the Act, carry the stigma of illegality. The Act therefore graciously extends legitimacy to hitherto unlawful associations. This has to do with the common law tradition to treat groups with circumspect. It explains, for example, why the common law is very uncomfortable with groups of

---

[4] cap. 54:01, Laws of Malawi.

[5] cap 54:02, Laws of Malawi. This Act generally regulates resolution of labour disputes through arbitration.

companies whatever form of control is adopted (Hadden, 1984). The law takes an acontextual approach and disregards social reality (Sugarman, 1990). When Parliament took up the task of legalising associations hitherto held as being in restraint of trade it appears to have suffered from the same myopia. The end result is that although legitimacy was conferred on trade unions, it is clear that the law has not come to terms with itself.

Although the Trade Unions Act recognises that a trade union is formed when members decide to form one[6] it nevertheless requires that such a union must be registered if it is to escape from the claws of the common law.[7] The legitimacy thus accorded upon registration of the trade union takes the form of 'rights, immunities or privileges' which are outlined in Part IV of the Act. These 'rights, immunities or privileges' are not available to unregistered trade unions which essentially means that they cannot operate without registration[8] and further they will be withdrawn when registration is cancelled. In addition the Registrar of Trade Unions can refuse to register a trade union[9] and can cancel registration of trade unions. These provisions, no doubt, were intended to keep trade unions within the arms of the state.

One of the grounds on which the Registrar can refuse to register or cancel registration of a trade union is if the trade union is used for any unlawful purpose.[10] Although such a provision appears harmless as it is, in that it is intended to ensure that trade unions are not platforms of crime, an unlawful object can be so widely interpreted that it may include activities which legitimately come within the purview of trade unionism. Take the situation where there is a trade union within an enterprise owned by the President or a trade union within the civil service and in both cases a trade union accuses the President of 'wallowing in luxury' while his employees or civil servants 'weep in poverty'.[11] These can easily be interpreted as seditious and render the

---

6 S. 9 (4).

7 S. 20.

8 This view is confirmed by S. 18 of the Act.

9 S. 15 of Trade Unions Act.

10 sections 15 (1) (c) and 16 (2) (d).

11 The quoted words were used by the trade unionist Chakufwa Chihana in "The Bumpy Road to Democracy" which though read as a statement in mitigation during his trial for sedition must have sounded clearly aggravating. See *Republic v Chihana*, Criminal Case No. 1 of 1992.

trade union a candidate for de-registration or act as reason for refusal of registration. Trade union leaders or officers of the union may be prosecuted.[12]

The Registrar can also refuse to register a trade union if it is "... not sufficiently representative of the interests ... of the employees in respect of which the applicants seek registration" or if in the opinion of the Minister it is not so representative[13]. That such a provision can easily be manipulated so as to avoid unions joining to form powerful bodies is exemplified by the struggle between the unions and the Registrar of Trade Unions in Malaysia. The Registrar was of the view that the electrical and electronics industry were different. They could therefore not form one union. The aim appears to have been to fragment unions so as to reduce their influence which if not checked would discourage foreign investment (Wangel, 1988). The Government also argued its decision was aimed at curbing undue influence of union leaders over uneducated work force who might join unions without making informed judgement (Wangel, ibid.).

It can therefore be argued that the requirement of the Act that trade unions be registered in order for them to operate while at the same time arrogating to the state the power to refuse to register or to de-register a trade union on arbitrary grounds is to give to labour with one hand and take the same away with the other hand. It ensures that the trade unions are firmly in the hands of the state.[14]

These concerns become much more pungent when it is borne in mind that in Malawi, as in most countries, the state is the largest employer and that a large number of enterprises are owned by political elites. The state and its functionaries have every reason to be wary of the existence of strong unions which would not only be demanding

---

12 See S. 59 (4).

13 See s. 15 (1) (l)

14 It may be argued that the registration requirement is against the Constitution of the Republic of Malawi and against the International Labour Organisation's Convention No. 87 concerning Freedom of Association and Protection of the Right to organize. Although this convention has not been ratified by Malawi, it is nevertheless part of law of Malawi since what it protects is contained in the Universal Declaration of Human Rights which is part of the Constitution: see S. 2 of the Constitution and *Chihana v. Republic.* MSCA CRIMINAL APPEAL No. 9 OF 1992 (Unreported).

improved conditions of work and hence reduce their profits but also political reform where this is seen as a *sine qua non* of any improvement in the welfare of labour.

It is because of the likelihood of trade unions taking their grievances to the political platform that most states in Africa sought in one way or another to contain the power of unions (Munck, 1988). In Malawi the strategy was not only legal constraints[15] but also integration of the Trade Union Congress[16] within the ruling party (McCracken, 1988) so that any anti-government policy would be checked from within. This political control has been the most effective tool of suppressing the labour movement. So that although the Trade Unions Act gave Malawians the right to form trade unions (and provided legal immunities from actions arising out of agreements in restraint of trade, torts committed by or on behalf of trade unions, conduct that induces a person to break a contract of employment or which interferes with the business of another, and avoided contracts which contained a condition that an employee should not join a trade union), the political control has earned trade unions the ridicule that they are "at their strongest, 'not aggressive' and, at their weakest, virtually non-existent."[17]

Thus the traditional purpose of trade unions to bargain collectively on behalf of their members has been taken up by structures created by

---

[15] Constraints include depriving trade unions of the right to enforce agreements which would be necessary for effective organisation. These agreements are: agreements between members of a trade union concerning conditions on which they, *inter alia*, shall or shall not be employed; agreements to provide benefits to members other than contributory or provident funds or pension scheme; agreements to pay fine imposed by a court on a member; agreements between one trade union and another (*see S. 23*). There does not seem to be any convincing reason why any of these agreements should not be enforced in a court of law other than that of making the organisation of trade unions difficult so as to render them weak and hence pliable by the state. It need not be overemphasised that the effectiveness of a trade union depends on its financial autonomy, ability to attract members such as by conferring benefits to them as well as proper coordination with other unions.

[16] It was the Government's wish to have the Trade Union Congress only as a trade union and the formation of trade unions was discouraged as far back as 1973. See File No. 4-1-2, Ministry of Labour Headquarters, Lilongwe quoted in Matembo Nzunda (1992).

[17] Matembo Nzunda, *ibid.* 8.

the state. The Regulation of Minimum Wages and Conditions of Employment Act[18] established the Wages Advisory Board in 1958 with the aim of giving power to Government to decide on wages policy 'as guardian of national interest'. Thus Government is able to keep wage movements consistent with economic growth. Further, there is the Wages and Salary Committee to which the private sector must apply for wage or salary increases of more than 5% per annum (World Bank, 1982, 37). It is clear that the state as the largest employer would not be keen to raise wages or allow other employers to effect huge wage increases. Further since the Government is run by elites who have investments, they are likely to advise wage restraints so that their profits can be maintained. No wonder real incomes have been falling.[19]

The absence of trade unions means also that there is little or no protection of employees' job security. Government policy towards this aspect appears to be based on the fact that it has at its disposal a reserve army of cheap unskilled labour. Not only can it afford to pay them less but 'the dignity and security of the Malawian employee does not feature very much in the Government's policies' (Kamchedzera, 1991:8). The Government's attitude is at best casual and at worst ambivalent. It merely states that 'minimum wages will be maintained where needed' and that a system of employee protection shall be maintained (Malawi Government 1987:179). The only legislation that would have accorded employment protection to workers in Malawi is the Employment Act[20] but this is very limited in application.[21] An employer can terminate an employee's services by giving requisite notice without assigning any reason for the termination. The fate of employees is therefore wholly left to the whims of the employer. It appears there can be no redress if the termination is based on grounds

---

[18] cap. 55:01, Laws of Malawi.

[19] Matembo Nzunda, op. cit.: 7, quoting World Bank, 1982.

[20] cap. 55:02, Laws of Malawi.

[21] It does not apply, according to the Employment Act (Application) Order, (GN 195/1964(N), to employees in Government service other than those designated as members of Industrial class (who are in general junior workers). It does also not apply to employees whose earnings (exclusive of commissions or other emoluments) are equivalent to a rate of or exceeding K 480 per annum. Low as Malawian salaries are, there are very few people to which the Act applies (see Kamchedzera, 1991). However sections 11 and 51–64 apply to all employees.

of racial, sexual or religious discrimination or even political discrimination[22]. A remedy is available where a summary dismissal is unjustified but here the attitude of the courts has been less helpful to workers. They have limited the range of circumstances in which summary dismissal may be held unlawful and have not shown any activism to depart from the common–law 'czar–self'[23] rule of awarding almost nominal damages based on what the employee would have earned had the requisite notice been given. In most cases therefore aggrieved workers do not sue except where the unlawful dismissal was accompanied by torts such as false imprisonment, malicious prosecution and defamation so as to enable them to claim higher damages (Kamchedzera, op. cit. 13). The lack of judicial valour to venture into new fields so as to afford a measure of protection to workers exploited by unscrupulous employers accentuates the plight of workers. But there are a host of other factors.

> I know of no case in which a court invalidated a contract by reason of gross exploitation, but neither can I recall a case in which a court was given opportunity of doing so. Exploited workers are not plaintiffs in courts of law – until the days of legal aid they had no access to the courts – they are not worth powder and shot (Kahn–Freund, 1972:6).

The judiciary is therefore not our best hope. They have to wait for cases to go before them. If poverty blocked workers in Kahn–Freund's England, here it crushes them. Our legal aid is not yet developed enough. It would appear therefore that workers can only seek a political remedy to remove obstacles to social justice.[24]

---

[22] Except probably employees whose contracts are regulated by statute and who might therefore apply for judicial review: See the case of *Chihana v. University of Malawi.*

[23] Kamchedzera, op. cit.: 13 points out that this stingy attitude arises from a clear antagonism between workers and the judiciary. See the High Court cases reviewed by Kamchedzera.

[24] See note 34 infra.

3. Labour Relations and 'the Economy of Affection': Control and Resistance

Almost all the labour legislation in force in Malawi was carried over from the colonial era[25]. The colonial state used this legislation to stifle labour resistance so as to maximise colonial control and surplus labour for capitalist development in the metropolitan state.[26] The common law applied was intended to serve this purpose. Malawi, like other LCDs, was firmly pushed into the 'old' international division of labour, where it serves as 'hewers of wood and drawers of water' for metropolitan interests (Stonemann, 1990).

The intransigence of the colonial state gave rise to nationalism. The labour movement was convinced that it could only better its conditions if the colonial state was replaced. A kind of partnership was thus struck between the labour movement and nationalists to work for a common goal. Thus the Malawi Congress Party instigated and supported labour strikes for political reasons. But when independence was attained, the state moved quickly to contain labour militancy (McCracken, 1988). Some of the first victims of the post–independence state were union leaders.[27] After this coup on trade unions labour militancy came to a halt. 'Peace and calm, law and order' reigned in labour relations.

A caution is however necessary here. Although there were fewer strikes in the late 1960s and early 1970s and almost none afterwards until the 1990s, labour resistance is not limited to strikes. There are forms of labour resistance that are more subtle and invisible than strikes, sit ins or lock outs. In Malaysia, for example, in Export Processing Zones, pockets of resistance have manifested themselves in form of mass hysteria leading to closure of factories for hours or days

---

[25] The post–independence state merely effected minor amendements. The only major development is the 1991 replacement of the Workmen's Compensation Act with the Workers' Compensation Act. See Kamchedzera, ibid: note 17.

[26] Malawi fared rather badly since it was treated as a colonial backyard where cheap labour could be obtained for mining and industrial development in Rhodesia and South Africa.

[27] Suzgo Msiska and Chakufwa Chihana were among them (McCracken, 1988).

(Adelman, 1990). Elsewhere in Africa and Latin America workers have resisted by absenteism, laziness, work as you earn, corruption and many other forms which may appear to be mere individual deviance but can be as damaging to economies as full blown strikes and are intended to reduce capitalist exploitation (Munck, 1988). In Malawi there has been no research as to what forms labour resistance has taken where the traditional forms are impossible. But if one goes by the inefficiency of our civil service and the corruption and embezzlement in our enterprises, one cannot help but think that workers have been making their voices known in various ways. There are a number of items sold on the informal market by small scale traders and street vendors most of which evade anti-smuggling legislation. These workers on the informal market and those who facilitate their dealings are fighting a system they consider is driving them under. Research is necessary to establish the extent to which this is happening and how much the state is losing. What we are able to say now is that these marginalized workers are victims of state repression but at the same time pose a real challenge to the state.

Rural workers have not been unscathed. More than 80% of the country's labour (ILO, 1990) is involved in agriculture and they are scattered all over the country's rural areas. They are unlikely to organise for offense or defence. They appear the most vulnerable to the machinations of a capitalist state. Those living on waged labour in tabacco or tea estates are unlikely to organise either because of the temporary nature of their contracts (most of which are seasonal) or because of their low level of education. Another major factor is the intransigence of the state already mentioned. Harrigan (1991) has admirably analysed the extent to which the country's ruling elite control the agricultural economy.[28] Those involved in subsistence agriculture (the peasantry) and in share cropping (or tenant) system have fared even worse in this scheme of things.

In a bid to drag the peasantry into the cash economy the state has attacked and weakened the survival base of the rural economy. The privatization of land introduced in 1967 under the Land Act,[29] the

---

[28] See also Matembo Nzunda, op. cit.: 8. He makes the point that there was in the 1970s a massive 'going into' commercial farming campaign 'to set examples to the ordinary people'.
[29] cap. 57:01, Laws of Malawi.

Registered Land Act[30] and Customary Land Development Act[31] was aimed at stimulating investment in land by providing title to land owners which would enable them to have access to credit. This has however enabled absentee landlords to grab land from peasants. Landlessness has increased. Most peasants have had to work in estates or take up sharecropping (Roger, 1981; Mhone, 1987). As population grows so does the reserve army of labour. Thus agricultural employers or landlords can afford to keep agricultural labour in appalling conditions. They have also taken advantage of the fact that there is no machinery to check the excesses of peasant exploitation.

Subsistance farmers have seen their ability to survive decline over the years as the monopolistic state marketing corporation (ADMARC) has extracted surplus value from them. Since ADMARC had been the sole legal purchaser of peasants cash crops[32] and controlled pricing of the crops and agricultural inputs the survival of peasants has been at the mercy of the corporation. The result has been that while peasants' real incomes have gone down, agricultural input prices have soared making it increasingly difficult for peasants to maintain a reasonable standard of living (Mhone, 1987).

Heyden (1980) argued that peasants in Africa have been able to escape or avoid the harsh elements of the influence of the state through the extended family and other interlocking community relationships. These relationships act as an alternative economy and provide individual supports of livelihood and social maintenance which in the absence of a formal social security system cater for those who are at the fringe of economic life. This alternative, the 'economy of affection', Heyden argued, gives peasants a measure of autonomy and acts as a buffer between them and the state. Heyden has been criticised on the ground that he overstated his case in that there was no evidence in Africa or elsewhere that peasants had achieved any independence from the state. The peasant has been taxed either through poll tax or on the market where state marketing enterprises extract surplus value from him. Moreover if he has to continue to produce

---

[30] cap. 58:01, Laws of Malawi.

[31] cap. 59:01, Laws of Malawi.

[32] See S. 6 of the Agricultural Development and Marketing Corporation Act, cap. 67:03, Laws of Malawi. Market liberalisation was carried out in 1990 to enable peasants to sell to private traders.

and reproduce, he must fall back on the state for farm inputs. This appears to be the plight in which the peasantry in Malawi finds itself (Hirschman, 1990). Further as a result of the increasing landlessness the extended family structures are breaking up rapidly as members seek means of livelihood in other parts of the country. The traditional bases of peasant survival are crumbling (ibid.).

However peasants have in their own way stood up against the oppression of the state. The introduction of new agricultural technology is one respect where peasants have resisted state policies. The improved maize varieties have been encouraged by the Government through the provision of credit facilities to purchase agricultural inputs. These varieties are largely grown for sale and hence the improved varieties would draw peasants deeper into the cash economy. But most of them found that while their debt was mounting, they had little in terms of food security. These varieties not only required adequate fertilizers but also pesticides hence increased expenditure (Hirschmann, 1990). The uptake of this green revolution has therefore been very minimal, about 5% (Lele, 1990; Chipande, 1987). The end result has been that some peasants would use the inputs meant for the improved varieties to grow the local varieties.

Further though the Government prohibited peasants on customary land from growing more profitable tobacco such as burley,[33] peasants have been growing this lucrative crop through either friends or relations who had been registered. Thus although the change of policy initiated in the 1990s to allow peasants on customary land to grow burley tobacco may be attributed to the World Bank pressure it was clear that the Government had realised it was going to be difficult to maintain such a policy which appeared to border on naked selfishness designed to suppress the peasantry. The peasants were already evading this policy through the economy of affection anyway.

4. Conclusion

The argument in this paper has been that the high handed approach of the state towards labour relations led to the suppression and demoralisation of both urban and rural workers. While a majority of workers

---

[33] See the Special Crops Act.

may not have seen the inside of prison cells as has been the case with most of those who stepped on the toes of the ruling party, the suppression of labour rights such as the right to organise and bargain collectively is as much an infringement of fundamental human rights as detention without trial. Workers sell their labour power for their own welfare. They must be allowed to freely negotiate a price for their labour either through collective bargaining or through a market which is not bent on extracting surplus value from them. Anything short of these is coercive labour and borders on serfdom. Workers were denied the right to negotiate the price of their labour and this caused deep resentment towards the state.

It is clear also that workers consider that they can only be given back their labour rights if a genuine political franchise is given to them. It is in this light that the wave of strikes beginning 1992 to the present should be seen. The banners carried by striking workers demand not only higher pay, but also replacement of oppressive management and political elites they consider obstacles to the improvement of their living standards.[34] The labour movement is not only fighting for economic rights, rather for a restoration of fundamental human rights of freedom of association and expression which the ruling party had suppressed for a long time. Labour rights can not be protected without these fundamental rights.

What of an agenda for the future? The state would do well to avoid seeking to control labour through patronage. Government's insistence on Joint Consultative Councils[35] as forums for resolving labour disputes cannot solve the country's labour crisis because it suffers from the same legitimacy problem which had hitherto bedevilled state structures designed to resolve labour disputes. Where it is possible to organise trade unions, workers must be allowed to set them up with-

---

[34] See 'Civil servants continue with strike despite government offering olive branch', in 'The Independent'. September 9-7 1993 p. 1 where strikers are reported to have demanded the resignation of the Minister of State in the Office of the President and Cabinet; 'Strikers demand Mama's K40m', in 'The New Voice', Sept. 6 - Sept. 12, 1993 (p. 1); 'The Mother of All Strikes', in 'UDF News', Tuesday Edition, 7th September, 1993 (pp. 1 & 6) where the strikers are reported to have gone on to the streets chanting slogans demanding the resignation of the government of Dr. Banda, John Tembo, Tendai Kadzamira and Dr. Ntaba.
[35] See the 'Daily Times, 22 October, 1993, pp. 1.

out state interference or prior authorisation. That way they will have credibility with the rank and file of the labour movement. Where trade unions are not appropriate such as where subsistance farmers and share croppers are concerned machinery should be set up to which these workers can complain and where their views can be respected. It is only organisations with grass root support which can reduce the labour malaise with which the state is faced.

References

Adelman, S., "The New International Division of Labour and the Exploitation of Female Workers in the Export Processing Zones of Malaysia", Coventry: University of Warwick, 1990.

Benedictus, R. & Berensson, B., *Labour Law: Cases and Materials*, London, Sweet & Maxwell, 1987.

Chipande, G., "Innovation, Adoption Among Female-headed Households: The Case of Malawi", in *Development and Change*, 1987, p. 337.

Cohen, R., "Theorising International Labour", in Boyd, R., Cohen, R. and Gutkind, P. (eds.), *International Labour and the Third World: The Making of a New Working Class*, Avebury, Aldershot, 1987.

Hadden, T., "Inside Corporate Groups" in 12 *International Journal of Sociology of Law*, 1984, p. 271.

Harrigan, J., "Malawi" in Mosley et al., *Aid and Power: The World Bank and Policy Based Lending*, London: Routledge, 1991.

Heyden, G., *Beyond Ujamaa in Tanzania: Underdevelopment and Uncaptured Peasantry*, Berkeley, University of California, 1980.

ILO, *Yearbook of Labour Statistics*, Geneva, ILO, 1990.

Kahn-Freund, O., *Labour and the Law*, London: Stevens & Sons, 1972.

Kamchedzera, G., "The State and Job Security in a Poor Country: The Case of ILO Standards and Dismissals in Malawi", Zomba: University of Malawi, 1991.

Lele, U., "Structural Adjustment, Agricultural Development and the Poor: Some Lessons from the Malawi Experience" in *World Development*, 1990.

Malawi Government, *Statement of Development Policies 1987–1996*, Zomba, 1987.

McCracken, J., "Labour in Nyasaland: an Assessment of the 1960 Railway Workers Strike", in *Journal of Southern African Studies*, Vol. 14 No. 2 (1988), p. 279.

Mhone, G., "Agricultural and Food Policy in Malawi: A Review", in T. Mkandawire, *The State and Agriculture in Africa*, London, Codestria, 1987.

Munck, R., *The International Labour Studies*, London, Zed Books, 1988.

Nzunda, M., "Two Models for Industrial Relations in Africa. The Case of Malawi" Zomba: University of Malawi, 1992.

Roger, B., "Land Reform: The Solution or the Problem", in *Human Rights Quarterly* (1981).

Southal, R., *Trade Unions and the New Industrialisation in the Third World* London: Zed Books, 1988.

Stoneman, C., "The Impending Failure of Structural Adjustment: Lessons from Zimbabwe", paper presented at the Annual Conference of the Canadian Association of African Studies, Dalhouse University, May 1990 (Mimeo).

Sugaman, D., "Some Major Issues in the Law of Corporate Groups", in D. Sugaman and G. Teubner (eds), *Regulating Corporate Groups in Europe*, Nemos for EUI, 1990.

Wangel, A., "The ILO and Protection of Trade Union Rights: The Electronics Industry in Malaysia", in R. Southall (ed), *Trade Unions and the New Industrialisation of the Third World*, London: Zed Books, 1988.

World Bank, *Malawi Growth and Structural Change: A Basic Economic Report*, Report No. 30A2A − MAI, February 1982.

5. The Pro-democracy Movement in Malawi: The Catholic Church's Contribution, 1960-1992

Joseph C. Chakanza

1. Introduction

The theme of this paper concerns a movement which is taking place not only in Malawi but throughout most of the African continent, Eastern Europe and many Third World countries, a movement in search of greater democracy. While the first liberation effort which reached its peak with the foundation of the Nyasaland Congress Party in 1944 was against foreign rule and sought political autonomy, the post-independent struggle is for wider human rights and liberties. Indeed the first liberation struggle was for collective self-determination, and now that this goal has been attained, the second struggle is for individual fulfilment. Whereas in Malawi, Zambia, and Zimbabwe and other parts of Africa, the two are separated by a period of about thirty years, in South Africa they appear to be going on at the same time.

2. The First Encounter

The contribution of the Catholic Church in Malawi to the process of democratization from 1960 to 1992 (before the issue of the pastoral letter) is generally regarded by many observers as not only negligible but insignificant as well. The popular view is that the Catholic Church broke its long silence and started making a significant contribution when the Catholic Bishops issued their epoch-making Lenten Pastoral Letter, LIVING OUR FAITH on 8th March 1992.[1] In my opinion, to concentrate only on the Pastoral Letter as if it were a bomb-shell that sent the country rocking, is to undermine the Catholic action and thinking which has gradually led to the issuing of the Pastoral Letter. I shall now turn to the Catholic Church's involvement between

---

1   Montfort Missionaries, Balaka, March 1992.

1960 and 1992 – before the issue of the Pastoral Letter – in matters which have a bearing on the process of democratization.

The first encounter between the Catholic Church and the Malawi Congress Party took place in October 1962 when Malawi News – the official organ of the Malawi Congress Party – made a vicious attack on the Catholic Church.[2] Mr Aleke Banda, then editor of Malawi News, devoted a complete issue to a charge that the late Most Rt Rev Dr J B Theunissen, former Archbishop of Blantyre,[3] was responsible for starting the Christian Democratic Party[4] to challenge the Malawi Congress Party. "To Hell with the Vatican Papal Empire",[5] he wrote in a eleven – page attack on the Roman Catholic Church as a whole and on Archbishop Theunissen in particular.

> If the Roman Catholic Church has not learnt any lesson from the religious wars that they have had in Europe and their expulsions from many countries of the world, they will be taught a lesson that they will never forget in this country of Malawi. They should remember that the African people of this country who are members of the Roman Catholic Church are Malawi nationalists first and if they have any allegiance at all to the Pope, that comes after they have performed their duty to their country.[6]

On the support for the Archbishop's stand, the article stated:

> We are pleased by one thing and that is that the Archbishop has not got the support of any other Bishop in the country. The Bishop of Lilongwe is a good friend of our leader Dr Banda.[7]

On church–state relations the paper said:

> We shall not tolerate any church to meddle in Malawi politics. The pulpit should be distinct from the political platform.

In response to this attack, the Archbishop and Bishops of Malawi signed a statement which was read both in English and Chichewa to

---

2 See Malawi News, 22nd October 1960.
3 Archbishop of Blantyre, 1950–1968.
4 Founded by John Chester Katsonga.
5 Malawi News, op. cit., p. 11.
6 Ibid., p. 118.
7 Ibid., p. 118.

members of their congregations during services on Sunday, 31st October 1960. The full English text read:

We, the Archbishop and the Bishops of Nyasaland, dismayed by the recent, unjust and un–called–for attack on Holy Mother the Church, on the Archbishop and on all the members of the Catholic Church, mindful of Our duty as Shepherds of the flock, wish to set forth to all the people the true position of the Catholic Church in Nyasaland.

Following the instructions of Our Holy Father the Pope, We, the Bishops of Nyasaland have not, do not and never will oppose the legitimate aspirations of the people of Africa; having so much at heart that this country of Nyasaland and its people be free, enlightened, prosperous and great, We fully encourage and sup–port their legitimate desires for independence.

However, We do not enter the field of mere politics. The Catholic Church should not be identified with any political party or type of Government but is willing to co–operate with any, provided it adheres to principles of charity and justice.

Human rights: But it is definitely Our obligation to make known to all the laws of God upon which every society must be built and to safeguard the human rights that have been given to all by God and which no ruler can take away from His people. Not only are we bound to advise on these laws and rights but We are also obliged to oppose any action contrary to them.

Therefore, We strongly protest against the accusation made in the Malawi News of October 22, 1960, that the Archbishop of Blantyre has formed a party. He has not and never will.

But, having been approached by a number of Africans, he merely followed his duty by advising them of fundamental laws of God and human rights, as he would have done for anyone else, regardless of their political or religious affiliations, had they asked him. We fully support him.

Love and Devotion: We also strongly denounce the false accusations against the Catholic Church in general, as made in the same edition of the Malawi News, while the doctrine and activi–ties of Our Church in the educational, cultural, social and charita–ble fields have clearly shown forth Our love and devotion to the people of Nyasaland.[8]

---

[8] "R.C. Bishops reply to attack by Malawi News, *The Nyasaland Times*, 1st November 1960.

61

While the tension between the Catholic Church and the Malawi Congress Party was still being felt, an Irish Catholic barrister from Blantyre, Frank Rooney, wrote to the Attorney–General, R M M King, urging that the Malawi News be prosecuted for its attack on the Catholic Church as the matter was in the public interest. In the letter he said "I am greatly affronted by the contents of the Malawi News".[9] In his reply, the Attorney–General indicated that he did not propose to institute proceedings in the matter as it was between himself and Frank Rooney and was entirely private. He refused to disclose the reasons why he would not institute a prosecution. Rooney would not be persuaded to accept the contention that the matter was not in the interest of the public to make known the reasons for a prosecution not being pressed. He reported:

> In all fairness to the Attorney General, I must say that he is not to blame. He is subject to the general and special directions of Mr Iain Macleod, the Colonial Secretary, who has in effect become the personal ruler of Nyasaland. In the pursuit of his earthly ambitions Mr Macleod is quite prepared to hold the Malawi Congress Party more sacred than the Church, and Dr Banda more important than God.[10]

Whatever [must have] transpired between the Colonial Secretary and the Malawi Congress Party so that the Attorney–General could play down the crisis is difficult to find out.

Commenting on the attack by the Malawi News, Archbishop Theunissen observed that:

> If the peaceful appearance of a new democratic party based on natural human rights and Christian principles has enraged so much the Malawi Congress Party, it can but be because human rights and Christian principles, justice and charity, are most inconvenient to them. Through this furious, unjust, and very low attack, the Malawi Congress Party has finally shown its true colours!"[11]

Responding to the same attack on the Catholic Church, John Chester Katsonga, founder of the Christian Democratic Party and himself a

---

9 "Take action demand is turned down", *The Nyasaland Times*, 25 November 1960.
10 Ibid.
11 "Malawi shows true stripe", *The Nyasaland Times*, 28 October, 1960.

Catholic, issued a four-page document.[12] He accused the Malawi Congress Party and its leadership of intolerance by being antagonistic towards his party and the Catholic Church. He emphasized that his party was channelling the nationalist aspirations along Christian principles and was not an affiliate of the Catholic Church. He predicted that if the Malawi Congress Party came to power and formed a government, the people would have just moved from one form of oppression by the whitemen to another by Dr Banda.[13] In a special communique, he expressed his sympathies to the Archbishop for all the insults against him by the Malawi News.[14]

Reflecting on this episode, we may note that the conflict between the Catholic Church and the Malawi Congress Party had no wide appeal both within the country and outside. No church within or outside Malawi ever voiced concern over the issue publicly. It was considered peripheral. This is so perhaps because the conflict was not on issues which affected many specifically. Given that nationalism was at its peak then, the encounter might have been seen by many as simply a show of strength between rival political factions. In such situations of conflict of interests or objectives, the use of abusive language, slander character- assassination, mud-slinging and intimidation helps to diminish the influence of the other. At the same time the would-be sympathizers would tend either to reserve their support or give the support clandestinely. The central issue was whether another political party besides the Malawi Congress Party could claim legitimacy and recruit followers. The Catholic Church was made a scape-goat because one of its lay members had sought advice on Christian principles of political involvement. The ordeal through which the Catholic hierarchy underwent served to safeguard its autonomy and freedom of expression on any relevant issue. By singling out the former Bishop of Lilongwe, the late Rt Rev Joseph Fady, as the friend of Dr Banda, a futile attempt had been made to drive a wedge into the hierarchy. However, the Bishops were as united as ever when they published their response to the Malawi News.

---

12 "Mau a mtsogoleri wa Christian Democratic Party: Kuyankha mtsogoleri wa Malawi Congress Party." Mimeo, October, 1960.
13 Ibid.
14 "Christian Democratic Party: Nkhani za padera", Memo, October, 1960.

3. Towards Nation–Building

As Malawi was drawing closer to self rule, on 20th March 1961, the Bishops issued a twenty–six page joint pastoral letter with the title: *How to Build a Happy Nation*.[15] This was in the aftermath of the conflict with the Malawi Congress Party. In the introduction the Bishops wrote:

> The events of recent months have provoked a certain amount of confusion in the minds of the faithful, confusion which is harmful not only to the souls of individuals but also to the steady and harmonious march of the Community towards freedom and happiness.[16]

The reason for issuing the pastoral letter is stated clearly:

> We the Ordinaries of Nyasaland, think it is our duty to put before you certain principles to enlighten and guide you in the building up of a happy community; desiring nothing better than that this country and its people should be free, enlightened, prosperous, great and happy ... Such is the spirit in which this letter is written.[17]

The letter dwells on the theme of Church – State relations. According to God's plan, man lives in three societies: family, church and state. Both state and church come from God: The former indirectly when God created man naturally sociable, the latter directly when Christ, its Founder and Head, delegated his authority over the Church on earth to St Peter. From this common origin, it follows that:

(a) Civil society must acknowledge God as Founder and Father and must obey and reverence his power and authority;

(b) Justice and reason itself forbid the State to be godless or to adopt a course of action which would be godless;

(c) The State has the duty to care for religion but cannot legislate on it. It has no right over the religious convictions of its subjects;

(d) The church must strictly admonish rulers to be mindful of their duty, to govern without injustice or severity, to rule their people kindly and paternally;

(e) Subjects to be obedient to lawful authority as to the ministers of God, binding them to their rulers not merely by obedience but also by reverence and affection.[18]

---

15 The White Fathers' Press, Lilongwe, March 1961.

16 Ibid., p. 1.

17 Ibid., p. 1.

18 Ibid., p. 11.

The Church and the State must cooperate as their functions, though distinct, are nevertheless complimentary. When conflicts do arise, there must be a mechanism to resolve them in order to secure harmony. Such a concordance of aims can be brought about only by a constant interplay or mutual sympathy as well as through friendly agreements. The Bishops then go on to deal with the vexed question of Church and Politics and end with a few hints to their flock on patriotism and love. They welcomed the coming elections as "a great step forward towards self-government and independence, the normal consequences of a nation's development." Whilst welcoming honest differences of opinion, the Bishops disapprove of intolerance, hatred or violence and have no objection to Church members joining political parties of their own choice. The Church as such is above political parties. It does not conceal any political aim or political activity under the cloak of religion. As long as the rights of God and the Church in all human activities – be they social, political, economic or religious – are upheld, the Church will not intervene. Although priests and members of religious institutes – ie, Brothers and Sisters – should oppose anything atheistic or anti-christian, they are entitled to hold personal political opinions and are allowed to vote in an election. However, the Church forbids them to take part in party politics. As for the Catholic layman, he may be a member of any political party that is not anti-christian. In casting his vote, a citizen should never be swayed by personal profit, religious or racial bias, but solely by this consideration: which of the conflicting issues or candidates is better for the nation. The interests of political parties should be kept subject to the public good. A good candidate is a man of proven honesty, moral courage true wisdom and wide learning; he should respect the family rights, the religious beliefs of the people and have a deep sense of his duties and social responsibilities. A citizen who is qualified to vote and does not use his right is guilty of a serious omission. The letter then goes on to deal with a Catholic member's duty towards his Church, his country and his neighbour. In conclusion, the Bishops state: "We send you this letter as a token of the heartfelt desire we have to co-cooperate in helping your country to become a nation of truly free men."[19]

In an effort to make the contents of this letter known and understood fully, a summary followed by a questionnaire was appended for dis-

---

19 Ibid., p. 25.

cussion and reflection in Catholic circles. Barely three weeks after the letter was read in all Catholic Churches, the late Orton E Chirwa wrote a review in the *Malawi News*[20] in which he described it as "a remarkable contribution to clear political thought in the country" and went on to say: "We in the Malawi Congress Party thank the Bishops for this clear statement, although we may not agree with everything they say". However, he observed that some of the theological tenets with which the letter dealt with were difficult to follow "especially to some of us who were brought up as Presbyterians".[21] He went on to state categorically that not every political scientist would accept the definition of a state steeped in theocracy. But all Malawians, be they Catholic, Presbyterian, Anglican, Dutch or Seventh Day will turn to the Pastoral Letter again and again for its political worth. The extent to which the Catholic hierarchy is prepared to co-operate with the future Malawi Government had been clearly stated.

For the Catholic Church in Malawi, this pastoral letter set the trend for its engagement in the affairs of the emerging political change. The fact that its contents were to be studied in the Catholic circles indicates that the Bishops wanted its followers to be versed in Christian principles in an African government. One reads between the lines that the tone of the first part of the letter is bent toward the formation of a state which is God-fearing. The main sources are Pope Leo XIII's social encyclicals: *Human Genus* (20 April, 1884); *The Christian Constitution of States* (Nov 1, 1885); *Human Liberty* (28 June, 1888). With the threat of aetheism and communism spreading in Europe, these encyclicals together with others, served to avert the danger, real or unreal, of the rise of atheistic governments. The memory of the conflict between the Catholic Church and the Malawi Congress Party was still fresh. What type of Government would the Malawi Congress Party establish? Some prominent politicians, like John Chester Katsonga, gave as one of the reasons for forming the Christian Democratic Party, the fear that if the Malawi Congress Party came to power, it would reject Christianity or at least would become anti-christian.

---

[20] April 13, 1961.
[21] Ibid.

4. In the Throes of Post–Vatican II Social Teaching

When Malawi became independent on July 6, 1964, the Second Vatican Council had already been in progress and only ended in 1965. This important event is used now to describe the state of the church as pre–Vatican II and post Vatican II. The Pastoral Letter *How to Build a Happy Nation* has been written in the pre–Vatican II era. Understandably it lacked the theological premise and pastoral practice of the post–Vatican II era and was based on an ecclesiological model by which the Church could still subsist without necessarily getting actively engaged in the social context of its day.

The opening paragraph of one of the greatest documents of the second Vatican Council, *The Church in the Modern World* (Gaudium et Spes) reads:

> The joys and hopes, the sorrows and anxieties, of women
> and men of this age, especially the poor and those in any
> way afflicted, these are the joys and hopes, the sorrows
> and anxieties, of the followers of Jesus Christ.[22]

This reflection of the Vatican II ecclesiology and social teaching emphasizes, as a starting point, on the social context within which the Good News must be proclaimed. This social context is made up of the joys and hopes, sorrows and anxieties of God's people, especially the poor. The commitment to the promotion of justice and peace is a constitutive element of evangelization. Recent Popes have developed this social teaching in their encyclicals. The 1967 encyclical of Pope Paul VI, *On the Development of Peoples* (Populorum Progressio) stressed the integral development of the whole human person and of each and every individual. This encyclical was followed in 1971 by *Justice in the World*, a statement of the Roman Synod of Bishops. It called for justice and peace education and action at local and international level, within the Church itself and in the wider society. On the African scene, the publication in 1981 of *Justice and Evangelization in Africa* was a milestone.[23] Catholic Bishops, religious and the laity

---

[22] A. Flannery (ed.), *Vatican Council II*, Liturgical Press, Collegeville Minnesota, p. 903.

[23] Symposium of Episcopal Conferences of Africa and Madagascar (SECAM), *Justice and Evangelization in Africa*, Mission Press, Ndola, 1983.

drawn from all over the African continent met to analyse the situation in their countries from the point of view of the biblical and Christian teaching on social justice and human rights. A passionate plea was made to urge catholics to mobilize themselves for the promotion of justice and peace.

In another encyclical, *On Human Work* (Laborem exercens) 1981, Pope John Paul II examined the problem of social justice from the angle of priority of labour over capital. Among the issues he touched upon were: democracy and participation, balance between public and private initiative; just wages and the importance of trade unions; human dignity, rights and duties; peace and international relations – to single out a few aspects.

A Pan-African Justice and Peace Seminar was convened at Roma University, Lesotho between 29th June and 3rd July of *Justice and Evangelization in Africa*. The communique issued thereafter gave a moving account of the plight of refugees, prisoners and victims of political and economic oppression.

Pope John Paul II's latest encyclical *One Hundred Years* (Centesimus Annus) 1991 has stated that:

> it is necessary for people in the process of reforming their sys-
> tems to give democracy an authentic and solid foundation
> through the explicit recognition of human rights.[24]

There is no doubt that the social encyclicals and documents cited above have helped to conscientize the Catholics into taking action on the plight of the peoples in Africa, particularly during this phase of the second liberation.

5. Towards the Second Independence

Africa in the 1990's has been caught up in a fresh blowing of the "winds of change" ushering in a "second" independence. Under the one-party totalitarian rule, important elements of society were increasingly being controlled by only a few people. Political power in practice became concentrated in the hands of a single leader and the ruling party. Despite the propaganda about being a "people's party"

---

24 See par. 47.

and promoting "participatory democracy", the reality has been that more and more people were not actually participating in political power in any meaningful sense. Human rights violations became widespread, all opposition was crushed ruthlessly and the independence and impartiality of the courts seriously undermined.

Economic activity, following a highly centralized socialist model, was mostly controlled by the state political interests and political personalities dictated the decisions on the processes of production, exchange and distribution. All aspects of the economy were dominated by large para-statals. Huge bureaucracies have developed over time, not infrequently accompanied by inefficiencies and corruption. While the masses suffered greatly from a declining economy, often the leaders became notoriously rich. Ideological thought has crystalized into "state philosophies" which are supportive of the system. Freedom of the press was severely curtailed.

However, today there is a move towards democratization and a rejection of the one-party system. Undoubtedly, the primary force for change has been the growing dissatisfaction of the majority of people with the inefficiencies and atrocities committed during the one- party rule. People have become frustrated and alienated, feeling that their voices were not heard, their concerns not paid attention to and their problems not solved. This frustration has been further exacerbated by the deteriorating economic situation in many African countries, with people being crushed under rising prices, absence or shortage of essential commodities, high unemployment rate, and the staggering social infrastructures and services of health, education, transport, communication, etc. Even if the leaders of the one-party systems were not to be held responsible for all these miseries, their lack of transparency and accountability to the people has made inevitable a serious challenge to their monopoly of power. These internal pressures for change have been reinforced by external factors prominent among which is the collapse of the Eastern European models of the one-party states to which the proponents of the one-party rule had looked for inspiration and guidance. In addition, pressure from the international donor community in Europe and North America was influencing change towards greater democratization. The protection of human rights and the promotion of democratic practices were becoming conditions for receiving aid.

In response to the disillusionment with the one–party rule, there is a felt move towards political democratization and economic liberalism. In general terms, political democratization is a movement away from the one–party rule towards multi–party democratic systems, free elections, constitutional defense of human rights, free press, etc. Economic liberation is the movement away from a centrally– planned state–controlled economy towards a free–market, privatised economy.

In this pro–democracy movement, the churches have played and are still playing an important role in articulating the people's grievances. In the absence of opposition groups which have either been banned or exiled, people look up to the churches to speak out on their behalf. In West Africa, in countries such as Benin, Togo, Congo, Zaire, national conferences have been chaired by prominent members of the church hierarchy. The challenging pastoral letters of the Bishops of Kenya, Uganda and Zambia have played and continue to play key roles in the movement toward democracy. The Bishops of Sudan have suffered persecution because of their courageous letters speaking out on behalf of their oppressed peoples.

6. The Lenten Pastoral Letter

Over the years leading to the issue of the Bishop's Lenten pastoral letter, *Living our Faith* the Catholic Church in Malawi had been preoccupied with the implementation of the decrees of Vatican II which had called for the restructuring of church institutions and renewal of church life in general. Developments were noted in catechetical and liturgical renewal. In social matters the Church had been heavily involved in educational, medical and other social services under the Malawi Government's control or supervision. The totalitarian character of the Government made it difficult or practically impossible for the Church to enter into any meaningful dialogue on issues affecting social services and the abuse of human rights. Yet the Bishops have not been totally silent. They did speak out from time to time in sermons and pastoral letters, criticizing the system and giving suggestions. In one instance Archbishop James Chiona of Blantyre told his congregation in a sermon that it was dehumanising and therefore inconsistent when people were forced to sing praises to the President on the supposed benefits he had brought them when in fact they were poor and struggling to make ends meet. Asked by the party officials to apologize, the Archbishop refused flatly, offering instead to take them to the poor of his Parish.[25] In Chikwawa, the burial ceremony of the Government minister, David Chiwanga who was killed in the Mwanza "accident" was conducted by Bishop Felix Mkhori, the Bishop of Chikwawa despite what the Government authorities had directed. The powerful pastoral letter of Bishop Mathias Chimole of Lilongwe Diocese, *Maso patsogolo* (Lit., Let us look into the future) 22 Nov. 1992 was indeed a follow up to the March, 1992 Lenten pastoral letter. These and many other isolated incidents in Catholic circles indicated that the Catholic Church in Malawi was not satisfied with the current state of affairs. What remained was to take a public and united stand on the matter. From 1990, the Bishops had been thinking of issuing a statement. Moreover there was a growing awareness among Christians that human rights are an integral part of the Gospel and that justice should be proclaimed and upheld. In addition, the changing world order and a growing movement towards democracy was being felt as exemplified by the developments in neighbouring Zambia, Zimbabwe and Kenya. When Pope John Paul II visited Malawi in 1989, he addressed the Bishops privately on the observance of human rights in this country. It was in these circumstances that the Bishops issued their Lenten pastoral letter *Living our Faith* which was read to all Catholic congregation on 8th March 1992.

It was an attempt to answer the question: "What does our faith and the Gospel call us to do today in Malawi?"[26] The letter called for dialogue on the issues of equality in wages and opportunity; participation in development, health care and education. Within a few days the Malawi Government banned the letter, declaring it "seditious". Many criticisms, insults and allegations were levelled against the Bishops. The Church/State crisis had started.

In an attempt to isolate the Bishops from the Vatican – a divide and rule strategy in which one can agree with the Vatican but not with the Bishops – the Malawi Government formally invited Archbishop Giovanni de Andrea, the Pope's special envoy, to come to Malawi to mediate between the Bishops and the Government. The Bishops were

---

25 *Moto Magazine*, May/June 1992.
26 "Malawi Follow-up to the Catholic Bishops' Pastoral Letter," AMECEA Documentation Service, Nairobi, Kenya, 15 June 1992, p. 2.

disappointed and troubled by this move. Since they were the ones who had written the pastoral letter they felt that the Government should not have by-passed them but should have dealt with them. Nevertheless, the presence of a Papal special envoy was regarded as a sign of solidarity. To clarify the position of the Bishops, the Papal Envoy suggested writing a memorandum in order to open dialogue with the Government. The Bishops accepted this suggestion but at the same time made the observation to him that such a text could be manipulated by the regime for its own ends. Here below is the full text of the memorandum that Archbishop G. de Andrea presented to the Life President on 7 April 1992.

> The Catholic Bishops of Malawi are concerned with the events that have taken place and are still taking place in the country following the issue of the Pastoral Letter, and wish to make the following reflections and observations in order to remove any misinterpretations that have arisen:
>
> 1. *It is unfortunate that the Bishops' concerns as expressed in the Pastoral Letter have been interpreted in a way that was not intended by the Bishops. The mission of the Church is to proclaim the Gospel and to help in the development of the Community of people in all respects.*
>
> 2. *The Church has always worked for peace and harmony among peoples, therefore any ill will, hatred or violence that has followed the publication of the Pastoral Letter is to be regretted. The Pastoral Letter is intended to guide, enlighten and invite the Catholic faithful and indeed all men of goodwill to respond in their lives to the teaching of the Gospel and the social doctrine of the Catholic Church.*
>
> 3. *The Bishops have neither the intention nor the interest to create tensions or confrontations in the Country, but to promote peace, justice and development in partnership. Therefore there is no way the Bishops could want to be disrespectful to His Excellency the Life President of the Republic, whom they hold in high esteem.* [27]

After the memorandum had been presented to the Life President, the Government issued the following statement:

---

27 *Ibid.*, p. 1.

The matter which arose with the publication of a pastoral letter by the Malawian Catholic Bishops now be regarded as solved. The problem resulted from discussions between the Malawi Government officials and a special Papal envoy from the Holy See, Archbishop Giovanni de Andrea. The Papal envoy expressed regret on the tension which arose after the issuing of the pastoral letter which was critical of the Government of Malawi and its leadership. The Archbishop assured His Excellency the Life President of continued respect and high regard for the Malawi leader by His Holiness the Pope and the Malawian Bishops. The envoy assured the Ngwazi that he had spoken to the Malawian Bishops who pledged their loyalty to him and that they do not want to disrespect him.[28]

Commenting on the Malawi Government's response to the memorandum, Monsignor John Roche, one of the signatories to the letter, said:

We had no intention that the memorandum should be interpreted as a retrograde step or an attempt by the Bishops to excuse themselves. When we wrote the Pastoral Letter, we simply wanted, as Pastors, to convey the Church's social teaching. For that, we don't need anyone's permission. What we were afraid of from the very beginning has in fact happened. After the memorandum, the Government first of all stated that everything was back to normal. Then they spread word that the Bishops had said they were sorry. Our Christians who initially welcomed our Pastoral Letter, were bewildered by this message from the Government. We could not accept this manipulation and we all agreed to contradict their interpretation of the memorandum. Then came my expulsion, an event which puts into question the Government's honesty and integrity.[29]

It is unfortunate that Archbishop de Andrea only stayed a few days in Malawi and therefore could not have seen for himself the use the Government made of the memorandum. However, Monsignor John Roche, after his expulsion from Malawi on Good Friday, 17 April 1992, went to Rome to report on what had happened and especially to present the view point of the Bishops of Malawi.

Support for the pastoral letter has come from churches and interest groups in Malawi, within Africa, from England, Scotland, United States of America, Canada and Europe. it will remain in history as the most pointed challenge to the Malawi Congress Party government.

28 Extract from *The Daily Times*, April 10, 1992.
29 Malawi: Follow up to ... *op. cit.*, p. 3.

With it the Bishops have lit a fire of hope for all Malawians that will be hard to extinguish. Many Malawians, no doubt, see it as a pathfinder, the first step on the road to true and genuine democracy.

7. Conclusion

In this presentation I have tried to show that the Catholic Church in Malawi has not just emerged from a "thirty-year silence on social issues" or from a "Ninety years of silent and acquiescent social conservation" to a responsible force for change – as some amateur church historians have made us to believe. Rather, the Church's social involvement has gone together with the "winds of change" blowing in Africa and within the Church itself. The call of the Second Vatican Council for a renewed involvement in the promotion of justice as a constitutive dimension of evangelization is an important dimension for the Church's active involvement in socio-political matters during this struggle for a second independence. In addition, the Vatican II ecclesiology which lays stress on the Church as the "people of God" not only calls for participation of the ordinary Christians in church affairs, but also for active involvement in working together for the betterment of their social, political and economic situation. In the 1960s the Catholic Church clashed with the Malawi Congress Party on the issue of the formation of a rival political party. The Church declared itself to be above party politics but maintained that it could only provide advice on Christian principles of political engagement. On the eve of the attainment of political independence from colonial rule, the Catholic Church issued the pastoral letter, *How to Build a Happy Nation*, a Vademecum for the Catholic Christian in which the Catholic hierarchy took a stand on Church/State relationship and set principles on how a Christian should engage in politics for nation-building. Although this letter had a limited appeal, probably because of its rather theoretical bent, it nevertheless helped the Catholic Christians to enter the new era with some sound principles. The 1992 Lenten pastoral letter, Living our Faith, actually translated the faith into action as it dwelt on relevant issues for which the people have been longing to articulate. Its appeal was instant, both at home and abroad. It has acted as mid-wife to the emerging political change towards participatory democracy that is taking place in Malawi.

6. The Law and Practice of Censorship in Malawi: a Critical Review

Fidelis Kanyongolo

1. Introduction

One of the most obvious functions of public law is the protection of the society from harm.[1] By using the specific context of the law and practice of censorship in Malawi, this paper intends to argue that if the function of law mentioned above is to retain its justification in a democratic society, there must first be a definite answer to the question whether law, rather than other means of social control, is the appropriate mechanism for effectively dealing with any given potential or actual harm to the society. Secondly, there must be clear and reasonable criteria for determining the harm envisaged in particular cases before the law is used to proscribe conduct which is allegedly harmful to society.

In the first part of this paper, we shall outline the statutory law regulating formal censorship in Malawi and discuss whether the censors, in the exercise of their statutory discretion, have successfully protected Malawian society from the harm which the statute envisages. In this regard, we shall not engage in any detailed analysis of the meaning of morality. For our purposes, we shall take it to mean standards of behaviour and social values which are held by the majority of Malawians and expressed as such by those social actors who are accepted to be the custodians of the values of Malawian society.

In the second part, we shall examine the relationship between the censors' discretion and the fundamental right of individuals to freedom of expression. Freedom of expression should not be restricted unless the basis for such restriction is not only reasonable but also clear in advance. In this regard, we will critically examine the wide discretion exercised by the Censorship Board and the Minister of Justice to determine whether the exercise of such discretion is guided by

---

[1] J. Stone, *Social Dimensions of Law and Justice*, London: Stevens and Sons, 1966, Ch. 6.

clear and reasonable criteria of "undesirability". In the final part of this paper, we will show that the changes in the law accompanying the current process of political transition in Malawi, indicate that there are improved prospects for controlling the discretion of the censor through the practice of judicial review of administrative action, and the emergence of a principle which requires statutes in Malawi to be consistent with the Republic of Malawi Constitution (1966) if they are to be valid.

2. The Legal Power of Censorship in Malawi

Formally, the statutory powers to censor publications and other forms of expression are vested in the Censorship Board (the Board) and the Minister of Justice (the Minister). Evidence suggests that these two censoring authorities coordinate the exercise of their powers[2] although they are granted their powers in two separate statutes independently of each other. The Censorship and Control of Entertainments Act[3] (the Act) sets up the Board and requires the Board to consist of at least five members, three of whom, including the Chairman, must be appointed by the Minister in his discretion. The Minister also appoints one other member "to represent other interested sections of the public, as the Minister thinks fit."[4] The Inspector General of Police and the Ministry of Local Government also nominate one member each.

The Board has the power, under section 24(1) of the Act, to declare that a particular publication is undesirable. The Board is required under section 24(2) to publish in the Gazette its decision to declare any publication to be undesirable. In practice, the Board also period-ically publishes a separate catalogue of banned publications which may be obtained by any member of the public. It is a criminal offence to import, print, publish, produce, distribute, display, exhibit, or reproduce any publication which the Board has declared to be unde-sirable. The offence is punishable by a maximum fine of K200 and imprisonment for six months and where the offence is a continuing one the offender is liable to the additional penalties of a fine of K40 and imprisonment for one month for each day on which the offence

---

2 Their lists of banned publications contain virtually the same items.
3 Cap. 21:01 the Laws of Malawi.
4 Section 3.

continues.[5] A publication shall be deemed to be undesirable if it is indecent or obscene or is offensive or harmful to public morals.[6] A publication shall also be deemed to be undesirable if it is likely to give offence to the religious convictions or feelings of any section of the public, bring any member or section of the public into contempt, harm relations between any sections of the public, be contrary to the interests of public safety or public order.[7] A publication shall also be deemed to be undesirable if it discloses, with reference to any judicial proceedings, any matter which is obscene or indecent or is offensive to public morals or any indecent or obscene medical, surgical or physiological details the disclosure of which is likely to be offensive or harmful to public morals.[8] Any publication which discloses certain particulars, as specified in section 23(2)(c)(ii) of the Act, in judicial proceedings for divorce, nullity, judicial separation or restitution of conjugal rights, shall also be deemed undesirable. In the exercise of its statutory powers of censorship, the Board has banned numerous publications.

Censorship powers similar to those of the Board are exercised by the Minister under section 46 of the Penal Code 8 which makes it an offence to import a publication which has been declared by the Minister to be a prohibited publication. The section does not indicate on what grounds the Minister may declare that a particular publication should be prohibited. This power has been used to ban no less than six hundred books, magazines, video films, printed textiles and recordings of music.

When the censorship powers of the Board and the Minister are examined, it is apparent that apart from indecency, obscenity and offensiveness to public morals, the grounds outlined in section 23(2) as the basis of a declaration of undesirability, are redundant since the types of expression which are "undesirable" under that section are already covered in the Penal Code by the offences of uttering words with intent to wound the religious feelings of others, criminal libel,

---

5 Sections 23(1)(a) and (b); and 32
6 Section 23(2)(a).
7 Section 23(2)(b).
8 Ibid 8 Cap. 7:01, Laws of Malawi.

sedition, doing acts that are prejudicial to public security and contempt of court.[9]

The relevant question for the paper at this stage is whether the use of the statutory discretion by the Board and the Minister has been effective in enforcing morality as such.

3. The Effectiveness of the Law of Censorship in Malawi

In Malawi, it is usual to justify censorship on the grounds that it preserves the society's morality.[10] This rationale raises the perennial jurisprudential question namely, whether morality can and should be enforced by law. This question was at the heart of the seminal Hart-Devlin debate which took place in the context of public debate in England on the issues of the legalisation of homosexuality between consenting adults in private and the criminalisation of public soliciting for clients by prostitutes.[11]

Lord Devlin was generally of the view that society's right to ensure its continued existence as a particular society justifies the use of all means, including the law, to achieve that aim. Criminal law can therefore be used to prohibit immorality which, if unchecked, would lead to the disintegration of society.[12] A close analysis of the list of publications which have been banned by the Board and the Minister reveals that the powers of censorship in Malawi have been aimed at ensuring that Malawians should not have access to books, magazines, films, recorded music and textiles that fall into three main categories: those featuring nudity and explicit references to sex, those portraying high degrees of gratuitous violence, and those which include positive assessments of communism or unflattering discussions of the Malawian political economy. In the light of the stated justification for

---

9 See sections 130, 200, 50 and 113(1)(a) of the Penal Code (Cap.7:01) and reg.5 of the Preservation of Public Security Regulations made under section 3 of the Preservation of Public Security Act (Cap. 14:02.)

10 President Banda said as much in his radio address to the nation on the Malawi Broadcasting Corporation on 31 December 1992.

11 See United Kingdom, the Wolfenden Committee Report on Homosexual Offences and Prostitution, Cmnd 247 (1957).

12 P. Devlin, *The Enforcement of Morals*, London: O.U.P., 1965, pp.9 and 12.

78

the law and practice of censorship in Malawi i.e. that it is to preserve public morality, we must conclude that the morality of Malawians does not tolerate nudity, explicit references to sex, extreme violence, communism and negative analyses of the Malawian political economy because these are somehow harmful to the society.

Professor Hart did not agree with Lord Devlin on the legitimacy of using the law to enforce morality as such. His view was that the law could only be used to proscribe that which was demonstrably harmful to the society. What is harmful to the society may incidentally be immoral but it does not follow from this that what is immoral is demonstrably harmful to the society as such. There is no evidence to show that immorality *per se* is a threat to the continued existence of society.[13] In deciding whether to criminalise an act, therefore, the crucial issue is whether the particular expression is demonstrably harmful to the society and not whether it is immoral.

Lord Devlin's view has been said to be based on a misconception of the nature of human society.[14] His argument suggests that moral per-missiveness necessarily leads to social disintegration. This assertion that society's continued existence depends on a constant moral basis is not supported by any logic or proof. No empirical evidence is offered for his central assertion that moral permissiveness leads to social dis-integration. It must also be noted that the law does not have any clear definition of immorality and lacks a mechanism for determining objective moral standards.

Lord Devlin's conservative approach also suggests what we think to be a futile attempt to fossilize moral standards and values which by their nature are dynamic. Morality is part of the social fabric which is constantly in flux and the law cannot hope to catch up with it, even with constant law reform.[15] In more general terms, Lord Devlin also asserted that law could be used to enforce morality because a moral society is in itself a goal worth achieving.[16] While we agree that a "moral" society may be a laudable ideal, we doubt that the best means

---

[13] H.L.A. Hart, *Law, Liberty and Morality*, Oxford: O.U.P.,1968, pp.9–10.
[14] R. Dworkin, *Taking Rights Seriously*, : London: Duckworth, 1977, Ch. 10.
[15] See K.N. Llewellyn, *Jurisprudence*, Chicago: University of Chicago Press, 1962, p.55.
[16] Devlin, *op.cit.*

to that end is through the coercion of criminal law.[17] If a society's basic institutions are not themselves grounded on sound values and ples, the coercion of criminal law is unlikely to establish the foundations of a moral society. Since we do not believe that there is a society which has found a formula guaranteed to ensure its survival as such, we are inclined towards a "free market " approach, which means that all moral standards, values and views should be given exposure through free expression and be allowed to compete in the market place of ideas so that those that are baseless should be unmasked by public scrutiny.[18] This includes matters of sexuality, violence and negative assessments of the Malawian political economy as well as positive assessments of communism.

Arguably, Censorship may also be rationalised on the basis that the standards that the censor enforces are agreed to by the majority and such standards must bind even the dissenting minority because the prevalence of the view of the majority is the guiding principle of a democracy. The law cannot accommodate all idiosyncrasies or depend for the definition of its scope on the subjective views of individuals.

In addressing this issue, it is important to examine the relationship between the idea of democracy and that of individual liberty. The former, in our view, does not mean tyranny by the majority.[19] Granted that in general there may be some practical sense in making the will of the majority the cornerstone of a democracy, we must, at the same time, realize that not only may the majority be wrong, but also that there are certain areas of individual human activity in which the view of the majority need not have a role. When the individual enters into the social contract, he or she does not place himself or herself entirely at the mercy of the state as a representative of the majority's interests. The individual surrenders freedom only to the extent that is necessary to facilitate the state's function of ensuring the secure and orderly existence of its citizens.[20] It follows from this, therefore, that the rest of

---

17 See Hart, *op cit.*

18 J.S. Mill, *On Liberty*, London: Longmans Green,1897; cf C.E. Baker, *Human Liberty and Freedom of Speech*, Oxford: Oxford University Press, 1989.

19 See T. Meron, *Human Rights in International Law*, Oxford: Clarendon Press 1984, p.173.

20 J. Locke, *The Second Treatise of Civil Government* (1690), J.W. Gough,

the individual's inherent freedoms must remain undiminished. We hold the view that the law and practice of censorship in Malawi in its present form is not capable of protecting Malawians from the subversion of immorality, if indeed immorality is capable of causing the disintegration of a society.

4. Censorship and Freedom of Expression

Even if one adopts Lord Devlin's position, it still does not address the second concern of this paper i.e. whether the discretion to censor in Malawi is limited sufficiently to safeguard the interests of freedom of expression and whether there are effective legal remedies available to those whose interests are adversely affected by the abuse of the discretion to censor.

Freedom of expression is widely recognized as a fundamental human right in almost all legal regimes and is not a luxury of Western liberal democracies.[21]

A number of justifications for the promotion of the right to freedom of expression may be advanced but the most obvious are: individual self-fulfilment, facilitation of social change through the interaction of ideas and views and the facilitation of informed participation in the democratic process.[22] The protection of freedom of expression is, therefore, beneficial not only to the individual but also to the society as a whole. It is, therefore, incorrect to analyse censorship simplistically as being a manifestation of tension between individual and group interests.

The fact that expression of thought is so important and is universally recognized and protected does not mean that unrestrained liberty presents no dangers to the society. The principle that laws that restrict freedom of speech are sometimes necessary in order to prevent harm

---

(ed.), Oxford: Basil Blackwell, 1946, par. 135.

[21] It is no longer a plausible excuse for ignoring human rights to argue that in developing countries,the need for development overrides the need to protect individual liberties. See *Foreword to Human Rights and Development*, D.P. Forsythe (ed.), London: Macmillan, 1989, p.ix.

[22] For a summary of the rationales see G. Marshall, "Press Freedom and Free Speech Theory", *Public Law*, (Spring 1992), p. 40.

to the society can, however, be abused to justify proscription of speech that is not demonstrably harmful but is merely unpopular or unorthodox. We suggest that in the absence of any evidence to show clearly what harm to society is likely to be caused by specific publications, the balance must lean in favour of freedom of expression to prevent the harm which censorship itself may engender. This harm includes frustration of individual self–fulfilment and interference with the free market of ideas and views which is the bed–rock of any genuine democratic process.[23]

Since freedom of expression is so desirable, it is important that Malawian legal institutions and theorists define the legitimate scope of censorship by: defining in clear terms the term "undesirable", stating what exceptions will permit the publication of material which is *ex facie* "undesirable", and setting out a mechanism for the control of the censor's discretion to prevent arbitrariness and inconsistency. Unless a clear line is drawn between that which is undesirable and that which is tolerable in the interests of freedom, harmful expression may be uncensored on the one hand while on the other, freedom of speech will remain under constant threat of diminution. The qualifications of the censors must also be critically examined in order to establish what special abilities a censor has that enable him or her to know what films, plays, magazines, pictures and books are "undesirable" by Malawian standards. The danger in having no clear criteria for censorship is that censors may abuse their discretion for example by taking into account irrelevant factors, acting in bad faith, using the discretion for improper purposes or by simply making unreasonable decisions. This danger will be considerably reduced if the law has effective remedies for those who fall victim to such abuse of discretion.

---

[23] In *Constitutional Law and Judicial Policymaking*, 2nd ed., New York: J. Wiley & Sons, 1980), J.B. Grossman and R.S. Wells report a study which showed that there may be a significant number of people who believe that pornography has benefits: 60% of a representative sample of American males and 35% of females found pornography to be informative, while another 60% of males and 24 % of females found it to be entertaining. Some feminists argue that pornography is entertaining mostly for men because it perpetuates their view of the female merely as a sex object: see Kappeler, *op cit*. and Mckinnon, *op cit*.

5. The Censor's Discretion, Judicial Review and Constitutionality

It might be said that this paper is exaggerating the threat to freedom of expression since the censor's discretion can be made subject to judicial review under s. 16 of the Statute Law (Miscellaneous Provisions) Act.[24] It may also be argued that any decision to censor, which interferes with freedom of speech, may be held to be invalid for contravening s. 2 of the Constitution and international law. Our view is that for a number of reasons, no comfort is to be found in these principles of legality.

In theory, it is possible to rely on the courts to protect freedom of speech from undue curtailment by a censor. Under s. 16 of the Statute Law (Miscellaneous Provisions) Act,[25] an application can be made to the High Court for judicial review. However, there are a number of practical reasons why resort to this procedure may not significantly protect freedom of speech from encroachment by formal or informal censorship.

One obvious weakness is that remedies that are available to an applicant for judicial review do not necessarily ensure that substantive justice will be done. Although judicial practice has been expanding the scope of judicial review to try and address questions of the merits of the application, the principle remains that an application for judicial review can, at best, address the merits of the case only tangentially.[26] It must also be noted that judicial activism thrives only in those cases in which the judiciary is bold enough to question the executive's assessment of the merits of a particular case. It has been said that the boldness of the judiciary in England, for example, depends on the nature of the issues involved in a particular case. In cases involving

---

[24] Cap. 5:01, Laws of Malawi

[25] Cap. 5:01, Laws of Malawi.

[26] For example, see *Associated Provincial Picture Houses Ltd v Wednesbury Corporation* [1947]2 All E.R.680,685 where Lord Greene,M.R. described the exercise of the power of judicial review of administrative action as "not that of an appellate authority to override the decision of the local authority but ... that of a judicial authority concerned, and concerned only to see whether the local authority have contravened the law by acting in excess of the powers which Parliament has confided in it." cf Chief Constable of North Wales Police v Evans [1982] 1WLR. 1155,

mundane issues like milk distribution schemes, dismissals of police officers and the allocation of foreign compensation, the courts have defined the role of judicial review more extensively[27] than in the area of civil liberties where "litigation has been dismally deferential to authority."[28]

During the current process of political transition in Malawi the judiciary has not shied away from judicial activism even in the area of civil liberties where the litigation created an apparent conflict between the judiciary and the executive. It is therefore reasonable to expect the judiciary to protect individual liberties in reviewing decisions to censor particular publications. On the other hand, the judges are likely to be influenced by the Malawian social context in which traditionally matters of sex and sexuality, for example, are rarely discussed openly and would be more inclined to sympathise with the restrictive censor rather than the broad-minded citizen.

Apart from seeking judicial review of the censorship of particular publications, it is also possible to test the constitutionality of censorship by applying to the court to declare that the statutory law empowering censors to ban or excise publications is unconstitutional because by curtailing freedom of expression, it violates section 2 of the Constitution which states that the Government of Malawi "recognises" the freedoms enshrined in the Universal Declaration of Human Rights.

Even if we assume that the law and practice of censorship are *prima facie* inconsistent with the Constitution, the next question is whether the power to declare the Censorship and Control of Entertainments Act or any other Act void on the grounds of unconstitutionality is within the jurisdiction of the courts. For an answer to this question, it is tempting to rely on the constitutional doctrine of parliamentary supremacy and assert that no court has the power to undo an Act duly passed by Parliament.[29] On the other hand it could be said that this

---

27 See for example *Padfield v Minister of Agriculture, Fisheries and Food* [1968] AC. 997; *Ridge v Baldwin* [1964] A.C.40 and *Anisminic v Foreign Compensation Commission* [1969] 2 AC 147.

28 See K. Ewing and C. Gearty, *Freedom Under Thatcher: Civil Liberties in Modern Britain* Oxford: Oxford University Press, 1990. See also J.Jaconelli, *Enacting a Bill of Rights*, Oxford: Oxford University Press, 1980, p. 179

29 See *Day v Savage* (1615) Hob. 95; *City of London v Wood* (1702)12

doctrine is not applicable to the Malawian situation because the Constitution of Malawi, unlike that of the United Kingdom, is written and should therefore be the supreme law which can prevail even over Parliament. As such, it may be more correct to use case authorities from the United States of America since they have a written constitution as well.

Unfortunately, there has been little, if any, development of a constitutional philosophy by the judiciary in Malawi. This may be because the courts have only rarely chosen to make authoritative statements on the Constitution even when the opportunity has arisen. One is therefore left to speculate on the Malawian cultural, political and social conditions which would necessitate the limitation of the content of the basic rights referred to in section 2 of the Constitution.

The absence of a clear constitutional philosophy in the judiciary and the judicial tendency towards narrow, textual interpretation of statutes does not give us much faith in the effective operation of the principle of constitutionality as a means of safeguarding freedom of speech from curtailment by unwarranted censorship.

6. Restructuring Censorship in Malawi

In the absence of any mechanism for effective judicial control of the discretion to censor, it is necessary to rethink some aspects of the law and practice of censorship in Malawi with a view to improving the protection of freedom of expression while at the same time protecting the society from harm which may be introduced through publications.

Our first suggestion is that the Board and the Minister should clearly establish what sort of immorality is considered so harmful as not to be tolerated in the free society which Malawi intends to be. Such immorality must be that which cannot be controlled by the marketplace of ideas and must present a specific, clear and imminent danger to the society.[30] The terms indecency, obscenity and immorality should not be taken for granted and require specific

---

Mod.669 and *Pickin v British Railways Board* [1974] A.C. 765.

[30] For an analogous situation in U.S. constitutional law, see the "clear and present danger" test in the cases of *Schneck v U.S.* 249 U.S.47 and *Dennis v U.S.* 341 U.S.494.

definition especially where, like in the Act, they may form the basis of derogation from a fundamental right.[31]

The second issue we must consider is whether censors are, in practice, equipped with sufficient expertise and experience to be able to identify indecency, obscenity and immorality in publications for the purposes of the Censorship and Control of Entertainments Act. We may also relate this to the question whether standards of decency and morality are national or local.

A more far–reaching proposal is that the Act be amended to provide for the decentralization of the practice of censorship because there cannot be national standards of decency and morality given the diversity of the society in Malawi. For example while it might be considered indecent for a female student to walk around bare-breasted in the corridors of Chancellor College, we found it to be perfectly acceptable behaviour at Tengani Refugee Camp in Nsanje. We suggest that the power of censoring publications be vested in the local authority of the area in which a film, play, record etc is going to be presented to the public. This would ensure that the censors' standards would reflect the sense of decency and moral standards of the people likely to be affected by the publication. Decentralization would not necessarily mean more expenses since the local authorities would use existing committee structures and licensing powers. At any rate, the authorities could, conceivably, still levy a fee to defray their expenses in the same way that the Board does at present.

The final aspect of the law of censorship that needs to be rethought is section 30 of the Act which provides that any person aggrieved by the Board's refusal to grant a certificate, licence or permit or attachment of conditions to the granting of the certificate, licence or permit, may appeal to the Minister and "the Minister's decision thereon shall be final and shall not be questioned in any court." We suggest that there should be a right of appeal from the Minister's decision to a court of law. Our view is that a dispute as to whether a publication is indecent, obscene or offensive to the morals is a dispute of law because its resolution relies on statutory interpretation. An error by the Board or the Minister in interpreting the statutory terms is therefore a jurisdictional

---

[31] Does "obscenity", for example, refer to that which causes shock and disgust or that with a tendency to deprave and corrupt the morals: see *R v Hicklin* (1868) L.R. 3 Q.B. 360, *R v Martin Secker* [1954] 2 All E.R.683.

error which nullifies the attempted ouster of the courts' jurisdiction by section 30.[32] Judicial review will also be necessary to determine whether in a particular case there is clear and imminent danger to the society which justifies the banning or excising of a publication even if its likely audience are adults. In an analogous situation where the issue was the limitation of freedom of the person on the grounds of national security, Mtegha, J. made a statement that deserves to be quoted extensively:

> "It is not enough, in my view, for the State to say 'certain activities prevalent in the City of Blantyre which posed serious threat to National Security and Public Order'. Far more information was needed in this case, and this is not just because the case is before the Court but because of fear of abuse of the [Preservation of Public Security] Regulations. As it has been pointed out on several occasions by this Court, the liberty of an individual is of the most sacrosanct." [33]

Similarly, since censorship is *prima facie* a limitation on a fundamental right, the definition of its scope should not be left to the executive branch of government. It should not be enough for the State, through the Board or the Minister to say a publication is indecent, obscene or offensive to the morals.[34]

7. Conclusion

The law of censorship in Malawi proceeds on a plausible premiss: that there are some expressions that cannot be permitted because they may result in harm to members of the society. The translation of that principle into the current law and practice of censorship as it stands now, however, does not adequately address the equally fundamental role of the law i.e. the protection of individual liberty from unnecessary abridgement by other individuals or institutions.

---

32 See Lord Denning in *Pearlman v Governors and Keepers of Harrow School* op cit. and Lord Diplock in *Re Racal Communications Ltd* op cit.
33 *In the Matter of Josephat* op cit. "present danger" test in the cases of *Schneck v U.S.* 249 U.S.47 and *Dennis v U.S.* 341 U.S.494
34 Does "obscenity ", for example, refer to that which causes shock and disgust or that with a tendency to deprave and corrupt the morals: see *R v Hicklin* (1868) L.R. 3 Q.B. 360, *R v Martin Secker* [1954] 2 All E.R.683.

The wide discretion which the censors have under the Act, engenders some practical difficulties, including the determination of clear criteria for determining whether a publication is likely to cause demonstrable harm to the society. Another potential consequence of the wide discretion is the likelihood of abuse of the discretion resulting in the diminution of freedom of expression. This real danger is heightened by the lack of a strong tradition of judicial review of executive action in Malawi and the general inadequacies of judicial review as a method of vindicating fundamental rights and freedoms.[35]

Unless, at the very least, the law and practice of censorship in Malawi are restructured as we suggest, the recent advances in the protection of freedom of expression gained as a result of the current process of political transition will remain on shaky ground, relying only on the benevolence of the Board and the Minister. If the current list of banned publications is anything to go by, any such benevolence is not to be expected tomorrow.

At a time when there is a lot of public debate about the nature and extent of freedom of expression in Malawi, the law and practice of censorship is overdue for a rethink.

Select Bibliography

Baker, C.E., *Human Liberty and Freedom of Speech*, Oxford University Press, 1989.

Devlin, P., *The Enforcement of Morals*, Oxford University Press, 1965.

Ewing, K. and Gearty, C., *Freedom Under Thatcher: Civil Liberties in Modern Britain*, Cambridge University Press, 1990.

Hart, H. L. A., *Law, Liberty and Morality*, Oxford University Press, 1968.

Kamchedzera, G.K.S., "Idea Communication and the Law in Malawi", unpublished seminar paper.

Wolfenden Committee, *Report on Homosexual Offences and Prostitution*, cmnd 247 (1957), U.K.

---

[35] See Lord Denning in *Pearlman v Governors and Keepers of Harrow School op cit.* and Lord Diplock in *Re Racal Communications Ltd op cit.*

7. The Experience of Women Under the One Party State and in the Political Transition

Peter Ngulube–Chinoko

Introduction

I would like to begin with a few remarks on the importance of theology. So many people feel that it is simply abstract thinking by special individuals, with little relation to ordinary life. But it is interesting that the Reagan administration in the United States decided on a policy to 'denigrate liberation theology', because they realised what a powerful force theology really is. In South Africa, Albert Nolan was asked why he wasted time on theology instead of getting into the dangerous area of the fight against apartheid.[1] To the contrary, he saw theology as quite dangerous, indeed radically subversive. The famous Bishops' Pastoral Letter of March 1992 in Malawi was no exception. It is with such a background that, prompted by the advent and introduction of multi–partyism in Malawi together with its accessories (freedom of expression for example) I have decided to venture into this topic 'The Experience of Women under the One–Party State and in the Political Transition' so that, as one prophet put it "What was done in secret should be proclaimed from the mountain tops."

The scope of this essay is limited. It is concerned only with exposing the sad experiences Malawi's women encountered under the one–party rule of the Malawi Congress Party. And again, very important perhaps, it also looks into the roles which women played during the transitional period from the one–party state to a multi–party state. The approach taken is mainly descriptive. Since the experiences encountered by the women are numerous, the problem of choice was inevitable. However, for purposes of discussion, these experiences have been grouped under the following headings: women's rights,

---

[1] M. Verteuil, "The Theological Background to Inculturation – LECTIO DIVINA" in *Catholic Biblical Federation*, Bulletin DEI VERBUM; Vol. 4, No. 26, 1/93.

threat of polygamy, health services and education, breakdown of morals, traditional dances and the CCAM. On their role during the transitional period, focus will be on how the women facilitated underground communication, on prison life and on the recent 'Operation Bwezani'.

1. Women's Rights

When we speak of human rights in Malawi, we cannot leave aside women's rights because, as has been rightly said by the North American women's liberation movement, the oppression of women is the oldest oppression in the world. Friedrich Engels wrote, "The first oppression of classes was that of the feminine sex by the masculine." And his disciple August Bebel added, "woman was a slave before slavery existed."[2] This situation is more spectacular in Malawi. From the rural scene, bent double under twenty–five kilograms or more of stout fuelwood branches, a woman staggers along a dirt road, her face stretched taut as a drum by the yoke tied round the forehead. By her side, her husband strolls erect, a *panga*, an axe or a hoe his only load. It is a typical Malawian sight, for in rural Malawi women are still the main beasts of burden. The practice here may have originated in the need for men to be ready to fend off the attacks of wild animals or rival tribes. The dangers have disappeared but the custom has been kept alive for male convenience.

This situation in Malawi was aggravated by the introduction of the one–party state in 1964. Twenty years after independence (1984), in the education sector for example, the situation in women's education was as follows:

64%	of females over the age of five had never been to school;
34,9%	had attended four years of primary school;
1%	had had a secondary education;
0,3%	were in their final year of secondary school;
6/100	of 1% had a university education.[3]

---

2 Esther & M. Arias (ed.), *The Cry of my People*, New York: Friendship Press, 1980, p. 82.
3 UN Economic Commission for Africa, *Women, Planning and Policy in Malawi*, 1984, p. 5.

In the same year 1984, women's participation in planning and policy making in Malawi was 0% This trend of events happened at a time when 52% of Malawi's population were women.

Malawi should learn from other African countries. Tunisia, an Islamic state, has in its constitution women's rights which are second to none in this continent of ours. In 1956, even before Malawi become independent, Tunisia promulgated a human rights code which ushered in the emancipation of Tunisian women. The code clearly proclaims the equality of men and women when it comes to exercising their socio-economic, cultural and political rights as well as their rights in a number of important aspects of family life. It seriously weakens the traditional preeminence of men. In its 213 articles, this code gave women rights they had in no other Arab country, such as the abolition of polygamy and repudiation, the introduction of marriage with consent, and equality of the spouses in the event of divorce.[4] Introduced in 1993, a security fund now offers divorced mothers a guaranteed alimony, a measure which places Tunisia far ahead of most countries generally regarded as leaders in the area of women's rights. The big question in Malawi at the moment is this: How far have the different manifestoes addressed this issue of women's rights?

2. The Threat of Polygamy

Polygamy refers to the union of a man with two or more wives. Much as it is outrightly condemned as a social evil, it is wrong to imagine that male lust or male selfishness is the principal motive behind polygamy. Men could satisfy their lust through adulterous unions and concubinage. Polygamy serves the prosperity and growth of the extended family, supplying a structure in which there are no needy widows and orphans. It also provides status and support for women in societies where they have no vocation other than marriage and the bearing of children to their husband's lineage. This was the practice, e.g., of the Ngoni of Mzimba district. In traditional society polygamy was the kindest solution in the case of a first wife's infertility. She would prefer to remain a first wife, rather than be divorced and be faced with the impossible task of finding another husband. It is sometimes even said that polygamy caters for the surplus women in soci-

---

4   Y. Lavoie, "African Women" in *MISSION*, September 1993, p. 6.

ety, ensuring that all are married. Of course, this is based on the assumption that all women have a vocation to get married. Notwithstanding these positive aspects, Christian teaching has traditionally taken a negative view of polygamy. Bishop Fulton Sheen of the United States once stated that "The secret of a happy nation and peaceful hearts is the realization that, in a proposal and in love, every man and woman promise one another something that only God can give."[5] In short, one man should have only one wife. In Genesis 2:18 Yahweh God said, "It is not right that the man should be alone. I shall make him a helper." In this case, a helper meant a wife and not wives. In Genesis 2:24 it says, "This is why a man leaves his father and mother and becomes attached to his wife, and they become one flesh." Becoming one flesh is a reality that can only happen between man and woman and not between man and women or between men and woman. Polygamous husbands admit that it is impossible to avoid partiality on their part and jealousy on the part of their wives. Polygamy further creates a family of considerable legal complexity. It lessens the educative influence of the father over his children and is irreconcilable with the educational and economic emancipation of women and the desire of women to play independent roles in society. Polygamy is also a major cause of desertion and divorce.

Sadly enough, the leadership of this country under the one party state as a matter of fact openly legalized polygamy, much to the detriment of the women. The legalization came at a time when 61% of those who have never been married were men, 89% of widows were women and 79% of those separated or divorced were women.[6] President Hastings Banda, who was the Life President by then, had this to say:

> Because I knew that as Inkosi ya Makosi, Christian or not, this is our custom, Inkosi ya Makosi cannot have one wife, no, and therefore, he has to have enough money and enough houses to support his wives. Why beat about the bush? We are Africans and we have our own customs, Christian or not. I can challenge anybody. I have read the Bible from the Old Testament to the other. There is not one passage in the Bible where they say *mitala* [polygamy] is wrong, no not one. (Laughter) Not one. I challenge any minister. Christ evaded the question. He did not answer yes or no. He said, "Over there there is no marriage, so

5 Ibid., p. 6.
6 UN Economic Commission for Africa, *Women, Planning and Policy in Malawi*, 1984, p. 1.

why worry?" (Applause) .... So if Jesus Christ himself did not
want to give a ruling, why should I give a ruling? As for Saint
Paul, he just evaded it, said, "Well, that is what Jesus Christ
said." He did not answer. Read the whole New Testament you
will never find Paul saying "*mitala njiheni.*" [Polygamy is bad]
.... And I am glad this morning to hand him keys, open the
house for him. The house has enough rooms."[7]

That is how the president of the one-party state interpreted the whole
question of polygamy. In any case, there is no woman who would
really like to share a husband. It is interesting to note that after the
president's speech, a few officers took second wives.

3. Health Education: the Lost Potential

Even after more than twenty-five years of Independence, Malawi
remains bottom of the league as far as providing health care to the
women is concerned. Because the education of the women was scan-
dalously neglected under the one-party rule, Malawi's women are
graduates of ignorance as far as maternal care is concerned. Death at
or around childbirth is all too common in Malawi as a result of this. In
the whole of the African continent, Malawi has the highest death rate
per 1,000 lives births as this table shamefully shows:

Death rate (per 1,000) 1985-1990[8]

Malawi	20,6
Somalia	20,2
Angola	20,2
Mauritania	19,0
Mozambique	18,5
Rwanda	17,2
Uganda	15,6
Zaire	14,2
Tanzania	14,0
Swaziland	12,5
Namibia	12,1
Zimbabwe	10,3
Mauritius	6,6

---

[7] Handing over keys to Chiefs in Mzimba District, Edingeni, Mzimba,
September 4, 1980.
[8] UN World Population Prospects 1990.

What is even more scandalous is the fact that countries which have been devastated by war for decades like Angola, Mozambique and recently Somalia are ahead of us as far as maternal care to the women is concerned. What the leadership and government of the one–party state did not realize was the fact that women's knowledge about nutrition, health and child rearing intimately affects the child's development. Ignorance about breast feeding, weaning foods or treatment for diarrhoea contributes to malnutrition; ignorance about sanitation can make the mother – as principal water collector, food preparer and house cleaner – the prime agent in the transmission of disease; ignorance about the beneficial effects of child stimulation can stunt the child's early mental development and lead to failure at school. If the one–party state had taken the priority of educating the woman, they would have educated the whole nation of Malawi.

What the next government can do to our women is that in health education and care, priority emphasis should be placed on pregnant and nursing mothers (including provision of family planning methods to allow them to space their next birth). Instruction on practical child care should be included in the upper years of every primary and secondary school curriculum, in teacher training programmes and in formal education programmes for adults, male as well as female.

4. Breakdown of Morals

> To be well with the one–party state in Malawi, the men adjusted themselves to two occupations: beer drinking and chasing women.[9]

This gentleman, a former over–zealous member of the Youth League of the MCP regrettably confessed that during the Party's Annual Convention in Mzuzu in 1991, he slept with over twenty different women. But the convention only ran for two weeks. Malawi's women became victims of prostitution under the party's playboys. There are countless incidents in which Malawi's women fell victim to sexual abuse under the one–party state. The writer of this paper at a time when he was a student at Chancellor College in 1988 recalls a very

---

9   Name withheld, Emfeni Burial Ground, 26/12/93.

embarrassing incident involving the 200 women from Kasungu who were on their way to Blantyre for the Mothers' Day celebrations. After having suppered at Chancellor College cafes, one young woman provocatively questioned the students:

> "Hey men, do your pencils have lead? Why do you burn your-
> selves by just looking at us like that? When we say we are free
> in Malawi, what do we mean?"[10]

Within a few minutes, all the nice looking women with the exception of a few old women vanished in the men's halls of residence for a 'familiarisation tour' as one student proverbially put it. As a matter of fact, most of these women were married. Hence, the fall of the one-party state was inevitable according to the late Italian Prime Minister Signor De Gasperi who stated that there is "no politics without morality, no state without a church, no democracy without religion."

5. Traditional Dances

Under the one-party state, Malawian women's involvement in politics to a large extent was limited to dancing for the self-imposed Nkhoswe No. 1. Women need to be involved much more in politics and community action at all levels to ensure that their perspective is taken into account. After all, few women's rights have been granted without being fought for first. Even under the organised dances, women have been harassed and intimidated in various ways.

> "We were harassed and called all sorts of names by the Youth
> Leaguers for not having put on the party's cloth during the
> rehearsals."[11]

Another pious woman of the Zambezi Evangelical Church stated:

> "Our Church does not allow us to dance for anybody save for
> God alone. Members of the MCP forced us to dance even on a
> Sunday, completely violating our inner conscience. At one
> time, some of us were actually beaten for having refused to
> dance on Sunday."[12]

---

[10] Chancellor College, October 1988.

[11] Scholastica Ngulube, Champhira, 15/11/93.

[12] Name withheld, Zambezi Evangelical Church, Chiputula in Mzuzu,

Another sad experience that was happening during one party rule was that accidents occurring because of party's functions were not made known to the public. MCP functionaries even commanded the bereaved families not to cry during such type of funerals. A case in point happened in 1988 when several girls of Northern Region secondary schools died in a lorry accident on their way to Karonga to dance for their Nkhoswe No. 1. One mother from Nkhata Bay whose daughter was among those who died sadly remarked:

> I was seriously advised by members of the MCP not to cry. I told the members that if a human being has been born with tears, there's no better moment to shed them than this. That was the beginning of my hatred for the MCP."[13]

6. Chitukuko Cha Amai M'Malawi

> In the CCAM gardens we worked like slaves. In the CCAM meetings we just listened and contributed nothing as if we were idiots.[14]

In its hey day, the CCAM brought more confusion than enlightenment amongst the women and men alike because there was already the so called 'League of Malawi Women.' Though ostensibly a women's development organisation, it operated in practice as an instrument of political control. It claimed to be charitable but the machinery behind the driving seat brought untold sufferings to the women. Women working in the offices used to leave their workplaces before knock–off time to attend CCAM meetings, much to the discontent of their bosses. Open criticism against the CCAM was equated with open criticism to the "wise and dynamic" leadership of the one–party state.

7. Underground Communication

> There are four creatures little on the earth,
> though they are the wisest of the wise:
> ants, a race with no strength,
> yet in the summer they make sure of their food;

16/12/93.
13 Name withheld, Nkhata Bay Boma, 18/11/93.
14 Sera Mnthali, Lilongwe, 23/11/93.

the coneys, a race without defences,
yet they make their home in the rocks;
locusts, which have no king,
yet they all march in good order;
lizards, which you can catch in your hand,
yet they frequent the places of kings." (Proverbs 30:24–28)

As the strength of the one-party state was very much boosted by the women, so too, its fall was very much brought about by the women. The women of Malawi proved to the nation that they were the wisest of the wise. They sang and danced 'NO' to the introduction of multi-partyism in Malawi. During the voting exercise, they sang and danced 'YES' to the introduction of multi-partyism in Malawi.

As far as underground communication was concerned, the women played an excellent role that was extremely risky. The opening words of wisdom unfold to us the role they played. Women had no strength to say no to the party's functions yet they were sure of what to vote for; women had no defences, yet they confided with their decided husbands; women had no queen, yet they cooperated well with one another; and some were invited into the palaces of the party's officials where they learned all their dirty tricks. The double-agents of Malawi. Bravo indeed.

8. Detentions

The tyrannical nature of the one-party state clearly surfaced in its treatment of the women who were detained and imprisoned during the transition. The best definition of the phrase 'violation of human rights' could be found nowhere else apart from the gaols of Malawi, by then, a one-party state. A woman office worker at the National Bank in Blantyre had this horror story to tell:

> I was interrogated by three men. They started questioning me about the paper. I said I know nothing. They started beating me with both hands clenched. He was beating me beside ears. Ear fluid came out of my right ear. He pulled my hair and made me fall down. He started stamping on my ears with his boots.... He pulled my clothes right up. He then took a pair of pliers and pressed the pliers into my vagina and pinching it with the pliers about ten minutes. I cried and cried. I started bleeding so I asked to go to the toilet.... He told me I was disturbing our President's mama and Tembo.... Then I felt pain in my jaw. I did not eat anything. It became septic. For two months I was

97

there in the prison discharging pus. I asked to see a doctor but was refused.... There were about 50 women in the cell in Chichiri prison."[15]

Another woman officer in Blantyre described her plight as follows:

"I was hit by a policeman's fist. I was hit on the leg. I was pushed into the wall of the cell. I was punched just above the nose and on my temple. I was punched under my left breast.... Then they ripped the clothes off me. They left me naked. They made me lie down. One pulled my hair. One pulled my legs. One man had pliers. They forced my knees and my legs apart. They started putting the pliers into my anus. I was crying at the top of voice. They withdrew. They sent me back to the Blantyre cells."[16]

True and genuine change comes through sacrifice and suffering. The women of Malawi underwent such trials. Some of the women who were detained were nursing mothers and lost their babies while in detention.

9. Operation Bwezani

If the incident that happened at the 'Gulf' in the city of Mzuzu between members of the Malawi Army and MYP sparked fire, it was the reaction of the women at Moyale Barracks that poured petrol on the whole incident. A group of Moyale women after having learned that the two soldiers had been killed are said to have preached to the soldiers in this language:

Don't you see that your friends are dying and yet you're doing nothing? Should your work be confined to solely removing our panties?"[17]

The disarmament of the MYP was therefore to a large extent perpetuated by the reaction of the wives of the soldiers. In this noble cause, the women played a part in saving the nation from the unknown disaster that was in waiting.

---

[15] "Human Rights in Malawi", A Report of a Joint Delegation of the Scottish Faculty of Advocates, The Law Society of England and Wales and the General Council of the Bar to Malawi–September 17–27, 1992 p. 24.
[16] Ibid., p. 21.
[17] The City of Mzuzu, 2nd December, 1993.

Conversely, the victims of the disarmament process have been the wives of members of the MYP. Destitute women with miserable looking children flooded the various bus depots on their way to their roots. One would be easily tempted to make the conclusion that the Jews' captivity and exile into Babylon was even more orderly than the flight of the wives and children of the MYP. They even lost the little possessions they had acquired. These women have a bitter resentment towards the ruling party and no doubt this will bring about a new direction of events during this transitional period. One woman, who preferred to remain anonymous, and who up to now does not know where her husband is, remarked pitifully:

> Will the MCP feed my eight children? Should we have to start our hell right on earth because of them? I will meet them during the general elections.

10. Conclusion

One thing remains evident in the paper. Women in Malawi have experienced more suffering than imagined. The common factor to all the hardships has been perpetuated by the government's denial of women's education in various fields. Worse still, women who up to now command a large population percentage are negligibly represented in planning and policy making in Malawi. All development plans, programmes and projects that could have an impact on women should be checked to remove any elements that might harm women's interests – or, indeed, to build in elements that could help. There is no space here to detail the more spectacular sexual and cultural iniquities that women in Malawi have suffered. The government should initiate programmes to help women. These could relieve family poverty, improve the quality of human resources, secure women's rights, reduce population growth rates, and ensure that women are represented in all policy planning bodies. Lack of development among women is a key link in the vicious circle of poverty. Perhaps this is the most promising place at which pressure can be applied to break the circle. Time has come for Malawi's women to step out of the shadows as they have proved during this transitional period that they can. However, the road that lies ahead of them is likely to be long and arduous.

8. Operation Bwezani: A Theological Response

James Tengatenga

1. Introduction

At about three o'clock early in the morning on 4th December, 1993, we were wakened by a volley of gunfire. It was the army firing at the Eastern Division Headquarters of the Malawi Young Pioneers some 300 metres away from our house.[1] As the day grew older we realized that this was the spillover of the Mzuzu revenge and part of Operation Bwezani (alias Operation Chitedze). As the events continued to unfold I caught myself saying, "Bravo Malawi Army". That response of mine to the country wide activity of the army unsettled me. Is it right for me to rejoice at the plight of the MYP and the "savagery" of the Army? "I am a Christian and a priest." That set me asking myself whether there is a Christian response to such happenings. In this chapter the attempt is made to briefly describe Operation Bwezani, look at its significance in Malawi's political history, indicate why it poses such a sharp question to the Church and propose a theological defence of the operation.

2. The action and the question

Immediately after the referendum the opposition and the MCP government agreed on the need to disarm the MYP. Five months later it was still not done. This was a cause of great concern to the nation and especially to the opposition.

---

[1] The Malawi Young Pioneers began as a youth wing of the Malawi Congress Party aimed at mobilizing young people to spearhead development, especially in agriculture. After independence it was soon subverted to become an instrument of political control, renowned for its brutality in stamping out any suspected "subversion". Later the MYP was heavily armed and became effectively a private army of the MCP.

The killing of two soldiers, on December 1, 1993 by MYPs after a tavern brawl led to events that turned the country into a virtual war zone. The army top brass advised caution, but the Junior officers and men "mutinied" and put the top brass under house arrest. They targeted MYP property and some MCP property. The army was bent on revenge: hence the unofficial name of the operation was Operation Chitedze.[2] The nation was poised for either anarchy or a coup d'état.

The captured MYP's were taken for questioning and subsequently released, however some fled across the border into Mozambique. Most of the arms were recovered but some are still unaccounted for. Secret files and dossiers were also recovered. The death toll was 25 (officially) and several tens wounded, some of whom were civilians caught in crossfire. The operation did not lead to the feared anarchy and neither did it turn out to be a coup d'état.

The heat of the event was over too quickly for the moralist, the church and those who are so inclined to issue official reaction. This is not to say that individuals did not react. They did, but neither the church as a body nor any branch of it made any statement. Some people were worried by the fact that this may be a precedent to some unwelcome interventions by the army. Others were concerned about the mutiny that was condoned. Yet others by the violence employed. Amongst this din of responses one did not hear a theological response. Does the Church have anything to say to this situation? Must it necessarily respond?

The MYP was paralysed, thus removing the menace. The army inflicted revenge. The citizenry was relieved of their bondage of fear. Most of the arms were recovered (some are still unaccounted for). This marked the end of the age of state terrorism of its citizenry and seeds of a "cleaner" youth department were sown. It also ushers in the possibility of cleaner politics. (i.e. politics without harassment by an armed wing of any party). The Army top brass was changed. More humane conditions for the Army are being put in place.

As for its significance I am persuaded that it ranks with the 1915 Chilembwe uprising and the 1959 Nkhata Bay shootings. It is also significant for the church as it challenges it to its self understanding

---

2 Chitedze is a hairy pod whose bristles cause the skin to itch and to flame into a rash when it comes into contact. It was also used for punishment.

on issues of violence: Does the end justify the means? Is violence always evil? Is it the case of "Good Friday" before "Easter?" Would there be an alternative? Must the church necessarily respond? What has this to do with the church?

3. In defence of Operation Bwezani

As indicated in the beginning, I am in solidarity with the Army in their Operation Bwezani. I do not see a contradiction in my being a Christian and priest on the one hand, and the support of this violent affair on the other hand. I believe that the imperative to love my neighbour and involvement and (as in this case) support for that which brings peace and a just order. Being a Thomist at heart I believe in some innate goodness in human beings, albeit flawed. Human activity in so far as it aims at doing God's will, consciously or unconsciously, is involved in the work of God and does so in obedience to his will. The operation was aimed at bringing about a greater good than the status quo and was a reaction to perpetrations of injustice. I condone the 'mutiny'. Augustine, Luther, Calvin and Thomas Aquinas held that when the choice is between obeying God and obeying man the former obedience is imperative. The top brass in the army and the government had lost their right to be obeyed. To do God's will in this incident was to be involved in what seems to be evil. With Bonhoeffer, I hold that it was the time "to put a spoke in the wheel itself", because not only was the existence of the state itself at stake but that of the church also. A peaceful status quo is conducive to the existence of the church. A papal encyclical puts it well:

> Where citizens are oppressed by a public authority overstepping its competence ... It is legitimate for them to defend their own rights and the rights of their fellow citizens against the abuse of this authority while keeping within the limits drawn by the natural law and the Gospels.[3]

If the Church understands its role as a prophet it cannot but give support, openly, to such an action. There, obviously may be some reservations as to some aspects of the Operation but if the church is one that not only lives in 'the times' it must also read and interpret 'the

---

3 *Gaudium et Spes* quoted in C. Villa-Vicencio, *Between Christ and Caesar*, Grand Rapids, Eerdmans, 1986, p. 122.

signs of the times'. It is not easy and the church may have interpreted the signs wrongly; but,

> Not to take a stand simply for fear of making a mistake, when others have more infinitely difficult decisions everyday seems to me to be almost a contradiction of love.[4]

> The church is called to be a "Watchman" in the midst of a nation, prophetically witnessing to the Divine demands for truth, justice and peace and against all forms of oppression, discrimination, injustice and corruption. For this task the church has a duty to be well-informed of what is happening in the nation.[5]

This is what the likes of Jeremiah and Elijah had to reckon with as they filed their minority report.

Some may object to the vindictiveness of the initial impetus. How can the church support the idea of vengeance seeing as it is God's prerogative? As a Thomist I have to study the intentions. Was the vengeance just for its own sake or was it for checking evil? A moral act is judged by its intentions. In this case the MYP was a menace and deserved to be dealt with accordingly, Says Thomas:

> Vengeance is lawful to the extent that its purpose is to check evil ... Reprisal for sin, consequently, should consist in depriving a person of the things dearest to him. Such things are these "life, soundness of a body, personal liberty and outward advantages like wealth homeland and reputation.[6]

and

> The controlled use of violence constitutes legitimate self-defence, for according to law it is legitimate to answer force with force provided it goes no further than due defence requires.[7]

Others may want to object to the apparent anarchy brought about by the operation. They may object to the looting. This cannot be avoided. In all cases of this nature there is going to be some lawlessness due to some criminal elements in society who take advantage of this situa-

---

4 Bonhoeffer quoted in *Between Christ and Caesar*, p. xxii.
5 *Between Christ and Caesar*, p. 176.
6 Aquinas, *Summa*, Vol. 41, p. 125.
7 *Ibid.*, Vol. 38, p. 43.

tion to their own ends. This is regretted but the good that came out of the operation outweighs this evil by far.

While some sections of the Church (eg. Christ against culture type) have advocated pacifism, most of the Church has accepted the use of violence but only where it meets the conditions laid down by the just war theory which states that,

> For a war to be 'just' it must (i) have been undertaken by a lawful authority; (ii) have been undertaken for the vindication of an undoubted right that had been certainly infringed; (iii) be a last resort, all peaceful means of the settlement having failed; (iv) offer the possibility of a good to be achieved outweighing the evils that the war would involve; (v) be waged with the hope for justice (vi) be waged with the right intention; (vii) use methods that are legitimate, i.e in a accordance with man's nature as a rational being with Christian moral principles and international agreements.[8]

Can Operation Bwezani be considered a justifiable military action when these criteria are applied?

The first requirement of this theory is that war has to be declared by a rightful authority. On this Operation Bwezani fails (not withstanding the face saving claims of the government when the operation was already underway). However, it was later owned by the state. The second has to do with the vindication of rights which have been infringed. MCP had no right to have a private army. With whom was it at war? As it turns out it was at war with its citizenry. It was an intimidation force whose task was to terrorise the citizenry into docil-ity. Its escapades are well known. The people's freedom was at stake, the government had gone over bounds. As said earlier it is legitimate to defend the rights. If it means doing so violently, so be it. The third has to do with war being a last resort. There comes a time when enough is enough. Two weeks after the referendum it was agreed to work towards the disarmament of MYP but nothing was happening. November came, parliament met but nothing was done about MYP. With the memories of MYP escapades during the run-up to the referendum, last resort or no last resort, something had to be done about it. Thank God for December 1, 1993. The fourth and fifth are related. They have to do with the outcome being good and on the side

---

8 Gill, Robin: *A Textbook of Christian Ethics,* Edinburgh: T & T Clark, 1985, p. 325.

of justice and outweighing the harm inflicted. The army was confident of victory and had the potential of wiping out the MYP. As for the outcome, very few casualties considering the scale of the operation. The top brass was decommissioned and a new one put in place and more humane conditions for the army were initiated, there is less fear among the citizenry of state terrorism (harassment and coercion) and the MYP has been Paralysed[9] and thus the grave menace removed. The last requirement has to do with whether the war is carried out in accordance with international conventions and dignity. In so far as can be seen the army targeted only the MYP and their property and some MCP property. This was a perfectly legitimate target. The MYP, for the most part, were treated well in that those captured were only taken for questioning and subsequently released. Surely a just end was achieved through just means. The church should support that.

We can also look at Operation Bwezani from a War of Liberation angle. In this it passes again. Its aim was to liberate the citizenry from a grave menace.

As a Defensive War it has to be a reaction to an unjust and actual attack. "Actuality exists when it [the state] is morally certain that the aggressor is making final preparations for an attack and does not desist in spite of sufficient warning."[10] From the rumours before the operation and from what the operation unearthed we see that it was a justified defensive (or is it preventive) action. Secondly the aggressor should not be harmed more than necessary. In this again the army passes. Thirdly the prospect of success should not be at the expense of higher goods (ideals) than those defended. One may have problems with this last requirement. However, for me there is no contradiction. The mutiny and disobedience to the government was justified because by being turncoats the top brass and the government's double intention they forfeited the right to be obeyed. Justice and peace and an orderly society are higher goods than obeying such and obeying unjust law is immoral.

Furthermore, I said that the church has to respond to Operation Bwezani because it is a significant event in the political history of

---

9 There are however some fears that the situation is not as certain, the fear being that the armed MYP's who fled into Mozambique are regrouping to come back and terrorize the country.
10 Gill, op. cit., p. 368.

Malawi and for the Church's own self understanding vis à vis issues of violence. Significant events in people's lives demand attention especially from those with responsibility for the moral well being of society. The church is thus expected to either condemn or bless. Its responsibility is one of renewing critique and not of conforming subjection.

The church is a prophet. However, the church in Malawi has yet to claim its role as watchman for God to the state. It knows this too well. It also knows the fruit of its abdication of this role as the community from which the civil servants are nurtured on the Gospel imperatives:

> The unfortunate thing for the church is that it did not witness enough. It did not work closely enough with those civil servants who still thought themselves to be at least to a certain extent Christian. It did not know how to remind them of the limits of their power and the danger of their abuses, not only for them but also for the civilization of which they were representatives and for the Church of which they are members.[11]

However, this need not stop the church from responding. It need not to be afraid of the fingers that point at its weaknesses. It need not pity itself and grovel in remorse without rising up to face the challenge. Someone said to the church:

> We, dare not be overcome by impotence, nor is confession of sin sufficient. We are called to repentance, relocating ourselves on the side of those who suffer most – in resistance, action, intercession and compassionate solidarity.[12]

In the Malawian situation it is necessary for the church to take responsibility for society. To borrow Richard Niebuhr's typology of church–society relations, it needs to combine the strengths of the *Christ of Culture* model and the *Christ the Transformer of Culture* model.[13] The former sees the church as involved in and with the struggles of the people and identifies closely with their cause. The latter regards the world as in need of conversion and reconciliation and sees itself as God's representative whose responsibility is to discern and ensure the enactment of God's law in society. A position

---

11 *Between Christ and Caesar*, p. 171.
12 Villa-Vincencio, *Civil Disobedience and Beyond*, Grand Rapids, Eerdmans, 1990, p. 85.
13 See H.R. Niebuhr, *Christ and Culture*, New York: Harper & Row, 1951.

which is akin to these two models would cause the church, in the last resort, to give its blessing to the use of violence. The church has to throw the state back on its responsibilities and aide the victims of state action. It is a pity that the president beat the church to it. He has established a fund for the victims. The church is also called to be a Good Samaritan (Luke 12: 25–37).

As it sees 'Jerusalem' self–destructing for not knowing the 'things that make for peace' (cf. Luke 19: 41–44 and Luke 13:34–35) it must move towards gathering her children under her wings like a hen does its brood.

Not only should it respond as a charity and hospice, it should also respond with a message of reconciliation. This would sound like a contradiction. How can the church, in the same breath, support (if not sanction) violence and vengeance and talk reconciliation at the same time? Such is the scandal of the cross (as opposed to Yoder's under-standing) that

> Reconciliation cannot take place until conflict is brought to the open. When God reconciled us to himself, he did not do that by smoothing over the history of our estrangement. In Christ God organised conflict ... yet the conflict itself gives opportunity for a change, for repentance and new life. The "Controversy of the Cross" is the very means of reconciliation and without it reconciliation could not be made complete.[14]

Thus Operation Bwezani may be seen as the "Good Friday" before "Easter". The church has thus, the responsibility of reconciling the citizenry on the one hand, with former MYP's and MCP, on the other, create and engender, in word and deed, a situation of acceptance. We are to love one another as Christ loved us. It is not reconciliation on the cheap.

Operation Bwezani was a necessary step on the path to national reconciliation.

---

14 A. van den Heuvel, quoted by B.Wren, *Nothing to do with Politics*, London: The Training and Mission Department, The Congregational Church in England and Wales, 1981, p. 20.

Bibliography

Andersen, H.C., *The Emperor's New Clothes*, Copenhagen: Scandinavia Publishing House, 1984.

Aquinas, T., *Summa Theologiae*, Vol. 41, 2a, 2ae, (ed. & trans. T.C. O'Brien) London: Blackfriars with Eyre & Spottiswood; New York: McGraw-Hill Book Co., 1972.

Aquinas, T., *Summa Theologiae*, Vol. 38 2a, 2ae, (ed. & trans Marcus Lefebure, O.P.) London: Blackfriars with Eyre & Spottiswood; New York: McGraw-Hill Book Co., 1975.

Augustine, *City of God*, New York: Penguin Books, 1972.

Bonhoeffer, D., *Ethics*, New York: Macmillan, 1955.

Bonino, J.M., *Doing Theology in a Revolutionary Situation*, Philadelphia: Fortress Press, 1975.

Gill, R., *A Textbook of Christian Ethics*, Edinburgh: T & T Clark, 1985.

Niebuhr, H.R., *Christ and Culture*, (New York: Harper & Row 1975 [1951]).

Sugden, C., *Radical Discipleship*, London: Marshall, Morgan and Scott, 1981.

Villa-Vincencio, C., *Between Christ and Caesar*, Grand Rapids: Eerdmans, 1986.

Villa-Vincencio, C., *Civil Disobedience and Beyond*, Grand Rapids: Eerdmans, 1990.

Wren, B., *Nothing to do with Politics*, London: The Training and Mission Department, The Congregational Church in England and Wales, 1981.

Yoder, J.H., *The Politics of Jesus*, Grand Rapids: Eerdmans, 1972.

9. Information Technologies in Malawi's Political Transition

Robert M Nkhalambayausi Chirwa

1. Introduction

Winning the support of the public is central to winning a political debate. Not only should the message get to the public in the most convincing manner but it should also reach a large proportion of the public. Newspapers, magazines, books, radio, television and video comprise the traditional media for reaching the public with a political debate. The party in power attempts to control the traditional media so that only positive aspects of the activities of the party are heard and known by the public.

The advancement of non traditional means of communication has empowered the ordinary member of the public. Communication and information technologies have played a big role in the advancement. New technologies such as the facsimile, the photocopier, and electronic mail have given an alternative to traditional media. As a result, the voiceless have obtained their voice and democracies have been enhanced. And these technologies have been made possible by the computer.

2. The Global Village

2.1 Impact of communication technologies on democracy

The coup attempt in the then Soviet Union in December 1991 against Gorbachev failed. Among the factors that contributed to the failure of the coup attempt was electronic mail.[1] The perpetrators of the coup were announcing that Gorbachev was ill and that the whole country was behind them through the official media such as radio, television and newspapers. Little were they aware that a network of computer

---

[1] T.S. Perry, *IEEE Spectrum* October 1992, pp. 30–32, "Forces for Social Change", IEEE, New York, 1992.

communications was causing unforeseen damage to their plans. Messages originating from a computer situated inside Russia's parliament were sent to all parts of the world explaining the true situation in the Soviet Union. The same computer inside Russia's parliament was being used to receive messages of support for the coup resistance movement from Western governments and other supporters. The received messages were then transmitted to other computers within the Soviet Union. Thus when the coup failed, the unofficial electronic mail was hailed. The controlled official media failed.

At the extreme opposite, the students' prodemocracy demonstrations in China at Tiananmen Square in 1989 were put down with a heavy hand by the communist authorities. Not many electronic mail facilities were in place in China at the time of the demonstrations.[2] It was difficult for the prodemocracy movement to give a complete picture of their cause to the outside world and for them to get encouragement from the knowledge of outside world support. The official media assisted in muzzling out the truth and in enabling the forces against change to win over the forces for change. However, the prodemocracy movement made some gains by the use of the fax. John Gage, director of the science for Sun Microsystems, Mountain View California said of the use of fax in the People's Republic of China at that time:

> Fax had a lot of power. A copy of a news article, with the *New York Times* banner, has more *eclat*.

The expatriate Chinese outside China were sending faxes to any fax number they knew in China. The senders of faxes changed recipient numbers since recipients of forbidden information risked arrest. When the information was received it was stripped of sender's name and fax number and distributed.

2.2 Bridging the gap

All over the world communication technologies have broken barriers previously impenetrable. President Clinton of the United States of America is more accessible to ordinary people than any of his pre-

---

2 *Ibid.*

decessors.[3] The President carries a computer with him wherever he goes. The computer is used for reading electronic mail letters sent to him. Of course most of the letters are read by his assistants at the White House but when he has time he attends to some of them himself. Electronic mail also makes a wealth of information from all over the world available to whoever needs it in any other part of the world.[4] As a result, people in one corner of the world easily know the activities of people in another. The world has truly become a global village. Quoting from the Institute of Electrical and Electronics Engineers *Spectrum* of October 1992:

> Today computers hitched by globe–girdling communications lines link a domain that is freed of time, distance, and political boundaries, made possible by electronic mail messages ... a U.S. resident cannot make a phone call to Cuba or travel there directly .... But if a person knows a Cuban's electronic name and address, he or she can send messages there. "

2.3 How information technologies work

Fax machines, photocopiers and electronic mail facilities duplicate information at a fast and cheap rate. The fax derives its power from the ability to send a document to many destinations just by dialing the numbers of the intended recipients. Electronic mail is similarly powerful in enabling communication but transfers information from computer to computer. Apart from ease of duplication and transmission of documents by means of these technologies, they have an added advantage of transmitting information to an absent recipient. The parties using these technologies may also agree upon standard codes which are unknown to authorities mainly because of the relative modernity of the technologies. When the documents are received, many copies may be cheaply produced with the photocopier for distribution. The photocopier also duplicates any other interesting information at the touch of a button. But even the traditional media has been revolutionised with the ubiquity of the computer. With desk

---

3   T.S. Perry, "Forces for Social Change"; W. Kanrowitz et al., "Live Wires", *Newsweek*, 6.9.1993, pp. 37–38; *The Guardian News Service*.

4   A. Dickinson, *Computers and Communication in Africa*, November/December 1993, p. 50, AITEC, Cambridgeshire, UK.; J.A. Adam and T.S. Perry, "E-Mail Pervasive and Persuasive", *IEEE Spectrum*, October 1992, pp. 22–23, New York: IEEE, 1992.

top publishing (DTP) which uses computers, more independent newspapers which can defy oppressive authorities have sprung up.[5]

3. How it was in Malawi

3.1 Good telecommunication but ...

Malawi has a good telecommunications infrastructure by African standards.[6] The communication technologies under discussion use the telephone network and Malawi is covered by such a network. By 1988 there already were several fax machines installed in the country. However, the Malawi government was also very efficient at controlling the use of this infrastructure. All communication devices brought into this country had to be approved by the Posts and Telecommunications Department. The government interfered with private telephone conversations. And even private post mail was opened and read by government agents.[7]

3.2 Controlled press and censorship

For a long time, only a few heavily censored newspapers and magazines were allowed to be published.[8] Any journalist who expressed views different from the "politically correct" was detained. And the "politically correct" views were not objectively defined so that entering into the journalistic profession was, essentially, taking a risk. The Malawi Censorship Board was efficient at banning books, music items, magazines, videos and newspapers. Malawi still has no television. Only a few printing presses existed and what they printed was monitored. When the political leadership of Malawi reached its pinnacle of power, the only radio station became a political tool. Malawi became isolated from the rest of the world due to lack of news. The government was attempting to keep the people of Malawi out of the global village. Malawi, as an isolated village, was to neither receive news from other parts of the world nor send news to other

---

5 J.J. Chienda, "The Role of Computers in Printing", *The Computer Monitor*, 9.3.1993, p. 7.

6 J.L. Lwanda, *Kamuzu Banda of Malawi*, Glasgow: Dudu Nsomba Publications, 1993, p. 155.

7 K.M.F. Kellyson, *Michiru Sun*, April 1993 p. 13.

8 Malawi Catholic Bishops, *Living our Faith*, Pastoral Letter of March 1992, section 11.

parts of the world unless it suited the government. There was even a move to stop people from listening to foreign radio stations such as Radio Netherlands, the British Broadcasting Corporation, Voice of America and Radio Republic of South Africa.

3.3 Restricted travel

Those travelling outside the country were viewed with suspicion. The government feared that such travellers had the potential of taking the well guarded news of this country to people outside the country and also the potential of bringing foreign ideas to this "perfect island". As a result, agents of the country followed Malawi nationals on foreign travel to monitor their activities and the people they were meeting. Even before going on a trip to a foreign country, permission to travel had to be sought from government.

3.4 Illiteracy

Illiterate people receive only the news that they can hear. The Malawi illiteracy rate is very high. Conservative statistics say sixty percent of the population of Malawi is illiterate.[9] This large section of the population can not reached effectively with the written word. Thus they are denied the news necessary to their existence.

4. The Right Time

4.1 Photocopiers

When the pressure groups campaigning for the end of the single party system of government in Malawi were working "underground", photocopiers were important tools. The news necessary for the campaign was typed on paper. Many copies of the document were made by means of photocopiers and distributed secretly, often under cover of night. Documents received from outside the country from human rights activists, exiles, and supportive governments pertaining to the campaign were also photocopied and distributed secretly. This

---

9   *Britannica Year Book 1992.*

unofficial news media was born out of necessity. The news items thus distributed were classified by the government as seditious documents and could not have been included in the official media without the editor of the newspaper facing detention and could also not have been distributed openly without the distributor facing arrest.

4.2 Facsimile machines

Contents of many documents from outside the country during the campaign for a multiparty system of government came through fax machines.[10] Fax enabled communication between the outside world and Malawi thus going round the problem of government interference in posted mail, telephone conversations, and publications. Some of the documents received contained condemnations made by major donor countries on the human rights record of the Malawi government. Copies of negative foreign newspaper articles on the Malawi government were sent by exiles. Human rights movements transmitted their condemnation of the government to pressure groups by fax. In turn, the pressure groups sent faxes letting the foreign movements aware of the dissatisfaction Malawian people had with the status quo.

The pressure groups then made copies of the received fax documents and distributed them all over the country. In this way, the fax and the photocopier stood tall in the transition process in Malawi. The fax and photocopier were to Malawi what electronic mail was to the former Soviet Union.

4.3 Illusory control

As more information of what was wrong with the government reached people, more Malawians began to question the government, and the underground movement gathered momentum. At the critical time when the question arose as to who would be the first to come in the open and challenge the government, its wrongs were pointed out openly by the Pastoral Letter of March 1992 authored by the Catholic Bishops of Malawi. It is interesting to note that the Letter was printed

---

10 B. Chunga, "Pressure Groups Strategies Working", *The Independent*, 26.4.93–3.5.93, pp. 4–5; Lwanda, *Kamuzu Banda of Malawi*, pp. 270–272.

in a press outside government control in Balaka. Shortly after the Letter was read, many of its copies were already photocopied and distributed around the country and faxed to key destinations such as the offices of human rights organisations and the BBC.

The government realised that some channels of communication in the country had slipped outside its control. During the crackdown on fax and photocopier operators in May 1992, the police were heard saying that they had been ordered to put an end to anonymous letters.[11] There was even a proposal to shut down telecommunications for a while. Implementation of such a proposal was impractical because it would bring government business to a standstill. Despite these attempts to control the fax menace, faxes continued to flow in and out of the country and there was a plethora of anonymous documents.

4.4 The Independent press

As wave after wave of pressure came, the government started introducing some changes. One of the early changes was to liberalise the press. Independent newspapers were allowed to be published. When the independent newspapers made their debut, many printing presses, fearing government reprisals, refused to print them. But this was not going to deter their influence. Modern printing heralded by desktop publishing is flexible. Most independent newspapers bought computers on which the newspapers were typeset (formatted.)[12] The editor–in–chief of the newspaper would then carry the formatted copy of the newspaper and go on a print hunting mission. When a printer ready to take the risk was found, they would just mass produce the newspaper. This method of producing newspapers is cheaper than the method of having the printer do all the working from typesetting to printing of the newspaper.

4.5 Effect on rural people

These newspapers and anonymous documents failed to have as big an impact in the rural parts of the country as they had in the urban parts.

---

11 British Law Society Delegation, *Human Rights in Malawi*, Report of September 1992 visit.

12 J.J. Chienda, "The Role of Computers in Printing", *The Computer Monitor*, 9.3.93, p. 7.

Their failure resulted from the high price of the newspapers which could not be afforded in rural areas and the fact that most of the newspapers and anonymous documents were in English – a language which can not be read by a majority of the rural population. The high price of the newspapers was due to high production costs and the fact that the newspapers had not yet started attracting advertisements. They were in English because they were targetted to urban people who could afford to buy them. Even if they came across a newspaper, rural people, most of whom are illiterate, could not read the predominantly English papers. After much criticism, most of the independent newspapers included a page carrying news in local languages.

Only the pastoral letter reached a wide section of the population because of the way in which it was distributed and released. On 8 March 1992, almost all Catholic parishes both urban and rural heard the letter read in English, Chichewa and Chitumbuka. By the time it was being banned it had already made a big impact. It derives its success from its well orchestrated preparation and distribution. The preparation and distribution was clandestine whereas the communication of its contents was open and at one appointed time of reading and making it public. The rural people also became aware of the activities of pressure groups through social contacts with town people. Due to the cultural practice of urban people maintaining frequent contact with their rural homes, ideas read from anonymous documents were transmitted to these rural homes.

5. The Future

5.1 Electronic mail in Malawi

Electronic mail has been introduced at Chancellor College and extended to other institutions in Malawi. This means people who are using these facilities have access to a wealth of information from all over the world. Subscribers are free to send any information to the network for whoever is interested to read. There is information on topics such as politics, environment, peace, science, religion, sports, technology, languages, law and many others.[13] Furthermore,

---

13 W. Kanrowitz et al, *Newsweek* September 6, 1993, pp. 37–38 "Live Wires"; A.

communication with resource persons contributing this information for anyone requiring further information on the topic is possible. The electronic mail facilities just installed do not provide all this information but enhancements are possible.

5.2 Required actions

This resource will however not benefit the ordinary people unless two issues are addressed. The first issue is to speed up the improvements in quality and number of telecommunication facilities. It is not desirable to have electronic mail facilities which are not reliable and fail to deliver information for a good proportion of the time. The second issue to be addressed is that of education. Illiterate people can not take advantage of sophisticated communication facilities.[14] Some argue that it is not wise to invest in technology at a time when conditions in schools and hospitals are poor. To answer this we borrow from Tony Jillings a communications consultant when British Telecom provided funds for a communications link between Peers School, Littlemore, UK and a rural school called Katumba in Tanzania.[15] Critics pointed out that the funds should have been used for basic amenities such as desks and chairs. He answered:

> It was not a choice between communication and a desk, it was a choice between communication and no communication.

The world we live in is a world of tough competition and people need to be socially empowered by better communication. Authorities will continue to stifle better communication because they are aware of the degree of empowerment the majority derives from it. But modern technology will not allow them.

Dickinson, *Computers and Communication in Africa*, November/December 1993, p. 50, AITEC, Cambridgeshire, UK; J.A. Adam and T.S. Perry, "E-Mail Pervasive and Persuasive", *IEEE Spectrum*, October 1992, pp. 22-23, New York: IEEE, 1992.

[14] K.Y. Lee, Former Singapore President quoted by *The Nation*, 17.1.1994, p. 4, "Advice from the Far East".

[15] A. Dickinson, *Computers and Communication in Africa*, November/December 1993, p. 50, AITEC, Cambridgeshire, UK.

6. Conclusion

Modern technology speeds up the process of democracy and development by enabling knowledge to be disseminated to all people. But technology is a tool. If a tool is not used it just wastes and does not benefit anybody. Only educated people can easily learn to use sophisticated technologies. Our leaders need to be committed to modern communication technology, computers and other forms of technology.

10. Church and Politics: The Case of Livingstonia Synod.

Fulata Lusungu Moyo

1. Introduction

Since the remarkable Roman Catholic Pastoral Letter of March 8, 1992, Malawi has seen and experienced a redefinition of politics. This redefinition has greatly affected the relationship between the Church and State. Livingstonia Synod of the Church of Central Africa Presbyterian (CCAP) also had to redefine its position as regards politics during this period of 1992–1993.

This article is a survey and evaluation of the position of Livingstonia Synod toward politics during the transition period of 1992–1993. How did this Synod define its ministry during this period? Was its involvement in the political debate during this period a lasting one or was it just a reaction to what was happening all round it? To present the full historical context we shall briefly trace how this Synod has adjusted its role and identity so as to "get along with" the successive historical phases of (1) Colonialism (1926–1959); (2) Nationalism (1960–1963); (3) Kamuzuism (1964–1992); and (4) Multi–partism (1992–1993).

However, it is of great importance to point out that though an over–all evaluation of Livingstonia Synod's position toward politics during different historical phases might seem to question the very prophetic[1] ministry of this synod, the prophetic endeavors of individual members of this Synod, lay and ordained cannot be denied.

---

[1] In the prophetic model, the church is distinct from the state but she lives with a continued responsibility for safe guarding certain Christian and human values in the society in which she finds herself. The church seeks to apply the subject of oppression and liberation in the Bible to the contemporary situation in society. She speaks out against oppression. She actively acts like the conscience of the society.

2. The Stand of Livingstonia Synod toward Politics during Colonialism (1926–1959)

It should be pointed out that Livingstonia Synod (then Livingstonia Mission) played a very significant role in bringing Malawi under the administration of the British Government in 1891. Yet it is the period after the CCAP was formed by the coming together of Livingstonia Mission, Blantyre Mission and the Dutch Reformed Church Mission in 1926 that is of interest in this section. Though Colonialism officially[2] ended in 1964 when Malawi became Independent, this period closes with 1959 when the Malawi Congress Party (MCP), which led the Independence struggle, was formed.

During this period, Livingstonia Synod was associated with a prophetic ministry through the likes of Donald Fraser and Robert Laws.

> ... the missionaries both encouraged the formation and influ-
> enced the character of the early native associations. Laws
> believed that to deny Africans the instruments of political
> expression was to encourage a radicalism that the Scots would
> be unable to control.[3]

Yet there was an ambivalence in the action of Laws in the establishment of the North Nyasa Native Association. While he encouraged Malawians to form such associations as a means of giving their opinion on what was happening in their country, he seemed also to encourage the Malawians to be loyal to the colonial government.[4] Laws looked on colonialism as a means to the realisation of development in Nyasaland, although still encouraging Africans to express themselves when necessary. On a similar note, Donald Fraser, an evangelist at heart – concerned mainly by the lost nature of the

---

[2] Officially Malawi became independent from the administration of the British Government in 1964 but practically up to this day Malawi is dependent on Britain and other rich Western countries and organisations especially when it comes to finances. This affects Malawi as a country on which policies to adopt and which ones not to adopt because usually with each aid and loan, there are conditions dictated by the donors or creditors.

[3] J. McCracken, *Politics and Christianity in Malawi 1875–1940: The Impact of the Livingstonia Mission in the Northern Province*; Cambridge: CUP, 1977. p. 257.

[4] Ibid. p 249.

human soul, did much to encourage the African expression and identity of Christianity in Nyasaland. Yet Laws and Fraser never planned nor carried out a Rising like that of John Chilembwe in 1915.

Probably what makes Laws and Fraser appear prophetic in Livingstonia Synod is the fact that they encouraged the Africans to be educated even up to University level and to develop an independent mind – expressing themselves freely. However, one would still argue that probably these missionaries did not consider the fact that this education would make these Africans go beyond bettering local conditions otherwise it becomes difficult to understand why they thought they could get away with their discriminatory mentality when it came to their insisting on being superior to these Africans despite their high education.

Though in strict terms, Livingstonia Synod seems not have been consistently prophetic during the colonial period, one realises that this Synod was more sympathetic to Africans than other white institutions. In many ways despite limitations, it was sensitive to the African's needs. Probably this is why it has generally been assumed that Livingstonia Synod was prophetic.

3. The Stand of Livingstonia Synod toward Politics during Nationalism (1960–1963)

Though the Malawi Congress Party was founded on 30th September 1959 by Orton Chingoli Chirwa and others, this period begins with 1960 when Chirwa handed the presidency of the above party to Dr. Hastings Kamuzu Banda. It ends with 1963 because it was in this year that almost everything about the independence of Malawi was finalized – even the Independence Day of 6th July 1964.

During this period, the Synod took it upon herself to support the Malawi Congress Party against the common enemy – the Federation of Rhodesia and Nyasaland (FRN). It did not worry about its stand at that particular time because, as far as it was concerned, the leaders of MCP and many of the other outstanding members were its children. Moreover, they still confessed their allegiance to it and the whole CCAP. It did not appear necessary to learn from the mistakes of the Scottish missionaries who had innocently aligned themselves with the imperialists hoping that by having Nyasaland under the administration of the British Government, slave trade would be abolished and Nyasaland would also be saved from the Portuguese influences – only to discover that the British imperialists had other agendas contrary to the missionaries' expectations.

This total involvement of the Synod during this struggle seem to be rooted mainly in the dissatisfaction of African Church ministers as regards the way they were treated – as juniors to the missionaries in decision making and other issues even though these ministers were equally educated or more educated than the missionaries. For as John McCracken (1977) puts it, lay missionaries assumed that wherever a whiteman was on a station, he ranked higher than the African even if the African was ordained.[5] Therefore, the Synod ministers wanted complete autonomy – to be their own bosses but they knew that as long as the British Government was in power, the missionaries would always be in power. The missionaries would still be very influential because the British Government would always rather relate with fellow countrymen and women rather than with African ministers.

Apart from the above reason, the African ministers and the MCP politicians were related in many ways. Most of them were former classmates at Overtoun Institute at Khondowe. Moreover, most of them also came from same home areas so with the extended family practice, they were relatives (kinsmen and women). So the joining of forces against FRN was like a family affair.

Unfortunately at this point in time, the Synod did not know that the way it related with MCP that time was going to have a lasting effect on the life of the Synod. The Constantinian model[6] adopted during this time turned the Synod and the whole Church in Malawi into an imperial cult with Banda as a kind of new messiah. So after

---

[5] Ibid. p. 249.

[6] In the Constantinian Model the church becomes integrated into a state or government which considers itself Christian. This model encourages the church to side with the ruling regime (oppressor) at the expense of the oppressed. The church, therefore, does not help the oppressed to stand up for their rights. She does not conscientise the people so that they know that it is their duty to work for justice and to change the unjust structures. (See J. Comby, *How to Read Church History*, Vol.1, London: SCM, 1985, p. 67; A. Kee, *Constantine Versus Christ*, London: SCM, 1982, p. 154).

independence, the Church had to live to please him instead of pleasing God and taking steps to help change the situation in Malawi.

4. The Stand of Livingstonia Synod toward Politics during Kamuzuism (1964-1992)

Apart from 1964 being the year Nyasaland achieved independence and became Malawi, it is also the year when first signs of Banda's dictatorship appeared as in September he dismissed three cabinet ministers who were joined with three other sympathising ministers resulting in a 'cabinet Crisis'.[7] This period goes up to September 1992 because although the watershed pastoral letter was read in all Roman Catholic Churches throughout Malawi on 8th March, 1992, MCP dictatorship continued in full swing until when the Public Affairs Committee (PAC) was formed in October 1992. Of course MCP intimidation continues up to now[8], yet its real sting seems to have lost its dangerous venom by the formation of PAC and other related bodies.

From the beginning of the Malawi nation (1994), the Churches fell prey to Dr. H.K. Banda's claims that he was a Christian – an elder of the church of Scotland. With Dr. Cullen Young, a retired missionary from Malawi, recommending him to the Presbyterian Church in Malawi, Banda won the support of both CCAP and other Christian churches in Malawi.

Like Eusebius and other pro–constantinian Christians, the Livingstonia Synod looked at Banda as God's provision for deliverance from the bondage of the FRN. The idea of Banda being a kind of Moses leading the people out of bondage to the promised land was not stated as given. But as one reads what the Synod wrote to Banda and as one listened to their prayers at national gatherings, one would pick up the implication in all these.

Because of what seemed to be unconditional support of the ruling party, the Synod had to pay highly over the years. It had to confirm

---

7 *Africa,* 1–31 July, 1964. p. 124B.
8 "Now" here refers to this whole period before the General Elections on 17th May, 1994.

the 'culture of silence'[9] by not addressing the real issues that affected the people publicly or even privately unless it was willing to pay the price – threat, torture and even possible martyrdom. To maintain this culture of silence meant that it had to dishonestly accept the MCP slogans based on half–truths and untruths: for example, according to MCP slogans: "Malawi has developed beyond recognition under the wise and dynamic leadership of Kamuzu".[10]

The Synod, therefore, was required to give the MCP regime its stamp of legitimacy and to restrict its ministry to personal spirituality and morality. But it was free from government control over its internal affairs. The Synod had to consciously pray for Banda and his government. Of course it is good to pray for our leader and civil government but the kind of prayers that it offered were a kind that made people like me refuse to say *AMEN* (Let it Be) at the end of them. Almost every Sunday, the person handling intercession would say:

> Lord, we pray for our Life President, Dr H. Kamuzu Banda that he will have long life so that the children of our children would also enjoy the peace and prosperity that we are enjoying in our lovely country today ... Amen.

In 1980, when oppression because more obvious in Banda's government, the Synod started sending what they called Loyal Messages[11] of which the following is a representative:

> We give thanks to God for the political stability, peace, and calm, law and order prevailing in the country. We give thanks and praise to God for the freedom of worship we continue to enjoy in this country under your wise and dynamic Leadership.

---

[9] During the MCP rule under Kamuzu Banda the people of Malawi were systematically denied freedom of expression. Discussing Malawi politics or even complaining of price increases on commodities was construed as sedition – punishable by detention without trial. Malawians were expected to thank and praise Banda for the peace and calm, law and order prevailing in the country and for its "unprecedented development." See R. Carver "Malawi Referendum: Free Expression Denied", *Article XIX*, Issue 12, April, 1993. p 3.

[10] *Hansard: Official Verbatim Report of the Debates of Parliament, Seventh Day*, 1st April, 1993, Zomba: Govt Printers, 1993, p. 1146.

[11] Rooted in the practice of the Church of Scotland where they send Loyal Messages to the Crown indicating their loyalty to the Monarch usually in response to a message from the Queen or King.

These favourable conditions have given us a unique opportunity to proclaim the Gospel of our Lord Jesus Christ freely. We pray that God may continue to bless our country, giving it righteousness that by His guidance we may play our role in promoting Christian love and understanding among your people in Malawi. We assure you, your excellency, that the CCAP Synod of Livingstonia prays for you personally, the party, the government and the people of Malawi so that justice and tranquillity may continue to prevail in our beloved land.[12]

Was the Synod trying to use this as a kind of bid for Banda's favours? The thing to note about this period is the fact that some individual ministers would stand up against MCP oppressive practices but instead of the Synod taking that as an opportunity to side with those courageous few and produce a teaching that would reflect the interests of the majority, the Synod suppressed those moves and instead continued putting their own interest as criteria of what to teach and what not to teach. Would it be too much to say that during this period the Synod was not guided by eternal perspectives – how to please God and fulfil his purposes on earth for the sake his kingdom? But rather it was busy making the life of the individual elite group of the Synod comfortable? Doing all it could to please the status quo so that life will be bearable: no harassment by the MCP political machinery – one wonders! So while to the people at the grassroots it appeared to separate politics from Christianity adopting the Lutheran Model, to the MCP Regime it approved of its rule as God given (Constantinian Model). Yet to other members of the Synod like Mama Nyamusukwa, the church during this period was carrying out its duties well.[13] The Church according to her is concerned with human's soul, money issues and other issues affecting the physical and social are cared for by institutions like the civil government. To her, the church would be losing her vision for God's Kingdom if she indulges in politics. So the ideal church – state relationship for her and those who think like her is Luther's Two Kingdom.[14]

---

[12] "The Loyal Message" in the Minutes of the Livingstonia Synod meeting, 8–13 April 1986, p.4.

[13] Mama Nyamusukwa is a church elder in Mzuzu, interviewed at Katawa on 2nd March, 1993.

[14] Luther's Two Kingdom Model advocates a clear distinction between Church and State. Both the Church (Kingdom of God) and the State (Kingdom of the World) were ordained by God but they must remain distinct from each other. The Kingdom of God is based on the Gospel and empowered by the Holy

5. The Stand of Livingstonia Synod during Multi–partism (1992–1993)

Though multi–party politics officially started on 14th June 1993 as a result of the Referendum vote, in this case I start with October, 1992 because that was the time around which Public Affairs Committee was formed – a committee which has worked so much in pressing for change during the transition period. The period can not however start with March 8, 1992 because even after the Lenten Pastoral Letter, the MCP government was still so powerful that it continued 'openly' to harass the opposition. The period closes with 1993 because, though the General Election was held on 17th May 1994, it was in 1992 and 1993 that the key developments occurred in the political transition from one–party to multi–party politics.

Despite the above periodization, it is of great importance to start the redefinition of Livingstonia Synod's ministry as regards politics from the Lenten Pastoral Letter. On 9 June a Synod pastors' meeting at Mzuzu called on the General Synod to act on the WARC letter.[15] When the full Synod met a t Khondowe in August, a Church and Politics Committee was formed. At this meeting members declared that it was the responsibility of the church to speak out in face of violation of human rights and social injustice. They noted the following points:

  a) It is a Church's responsibility to speak out on violations of human rights, good governance through the rule of law.
  b) The Church must participate in affairs of the community by being the voice of the voiceless.
  c) In view of the growing fears and violations being experienced by the Church through detentions and arrests of some ministers and security surveillance during Church Services, the committee recommended that the following be a plan of action:
  (i) The government be urged to call for a referendum in order to find out people's views.

Spirit. The Kingdom of the world is based on Law and the power of the sword. It is responsible to create the climate of law and order, peace and calm which allows for the propagation of the Gospel.
[15] "The Nation of Malawi in Crisis: the Church's Concern", Geneva: World Alliance of Reformed Churches, 2 June 1992, p.2; see above pp. 32ff.

(ii) Through General Synod, pressure be mounted for the formation of a broad based commission which should contact the Government from time to time.

(iii) Demand the release of remaining political prisoners in order for them to be tried in open court if found guilty

(iv) Broadcast the strategies of the Church on BBC. and with Church media in Scotland.

(v) Joint Sunday Services with other denominations be encouraged in all the congregations.

(vi) Peaceful demonstrations.

(vii)A Church and Nation Committee to be established which should discuss political issues" [16]

The above proposals in one way or another have been carried out. After the President's announcement of the National Referendum, the Church remained much involved in educating the people of Livingstonia Synod about the referendum process. Moreover ministers like Revs. Longwe, Chanda Mhone, Ted Mwambila, and Dr O.P. Mazunda have actually addressed political rallies usually organised by the then pressure groups like AFORD. In most cases what would have been possible hindrance to the Church's participation in politics before March, 1992, namely arrests by police and general harassment did not manage to hinder anybody. Some ministers and lay leaders were in and out of prison but such experiences just managed to create even more zeal among them. Many other people were inspired to go ahead with campaigns for a more democratic Malawi.

Daring sermons were preached and ministers paid for it by imprisonment and demoralising songs from MCP Women's League members and even Youth League. But "no retreat, no surrender" seemed to have become the motto. In face of arrests, the Church courageously denounced such practices by the government and little by little the government in most cases bowed to pressure:

> The Church of Central Africa Presbyterian Synod of Livingstonia strongly condemns the unjustified arrests and harassment of its ministers and lay people, vis-a-vis Revs Aaron Longwe, Winstone M Nyirenda and Jacob Kumwenda. We are deeply saddened that the government continues to harass and effect arrests of our church Ministers

---

16 "The Church and Politics" in Livingstonia Synod Minute of June 28 1992, pp. 57-58.

and lay people. We demand that this tendency be stopped forth with.[17]

The Synod started writing to the President addressing issues like the need to look into the record of human rights in Malawi and the need to release political prisoners like the Chirwas (unfortunately Orton Chirwa died in prison in October). Although we must weigh the motives of such a sudden and timely involvement, it is necessary to acknowledge that Livingstonia Synod's siding with the voiceless majority at this particular time cost it much pain. It was denounced by MCP advocates as not being Christian but having other agendas like wanting power politically. The list of the cost it had or still has to pay is unending. The willingness to pay the cost makes one identify this kind of involvement as prophetic.

Yet on the other hand one cannot avoid wondering whether Livingstonia as a Synod defined its prophetic ministry well enough as regards how far it could get involved and for whom. This comes to be a concern because this involvement by the Synod was intended to voice the grievances of the ordinary people. Yet at the same time it was at the expense of the rank and the file: the unavailability of pastoral care because the pastors/ministers were busy campaigning for a more democratic Malawi; and their having to listen to sermons denouncing Banda's oppression. Are the people not going to dry up spiritually? This prophetic model if not checked might lead to another Constantinian model in the next government.

6. Conclusion

Throughout the paper, it has been very difficult to give one definition on the position of the Livingstonia Synod vis-a-vis what was happening in the political realm. In general the Synod has been applauding the working of the MCP political machinery thus adopting the Constantinian Model. But trying to defend itself, probably knowing right well which stand God required from it, it has tried to justify itself by separating spiritual life from political life in a way adopting Luther's 'Two Kingdoms'. The question of course is – why has Liv-

---

[17] Statement on the Arrests of Church Ministers by CCAP, Livingstonia Synod, Sept 1, 1992. (St Peters Major Seminary, 'subversive file').

ingstonia Synod of the CCAP related to the MCP regime and to society as a whole in the way that it has done?

Between 1960 and 1963, Livingstonia Synod's close identification with the then fighters for independence, most of whom were in the Nyasaland African Congress (later MCP) can be explained as a natural thing seeing that the ordained ministers in the Synod were in most cases associates of the politicians. But from what independence (1964) has led to– oppression – can we trust the Synod that as it was plunging itself into MCP politics it had its ears tuned to God? Was what it was doing something that tallied with the Word of God? Or was it aware of the fact that time for change in politics had come so that, if it was to gain from this change, it had to align itself with the politicians who would matter? Did it not take the step it took, so as to have its interests preserved by what was to be the status quo – MCP? However, prophetic ministry calls the church as an institution to present the interests of the oppressed and make its teaching reflect the voice of these oppressed people: giving them hope, encouragement and momentum to take up their stand against oppression. The Livingstonia Synod Committee which is the ruling body for the whole Synod of Livingstonia has instead favoured the interests of the privileged few by remaining silent. By identifying with the MCP government from 1964 to February, 1992 this Committee had to adopt a culture of silence – deliberately ignoring real issues that affected the members of the whole Synod so that the latter's interests could be met: Did they not betray the Lord's cause – the poor, the downtrodden, the oppressed masses that constitute the majority of the Synod, so that all may be well with them as regards to MCP favours. Unfortunately there were not many favours since the Synod constitutes the North which turned out to be the outcast of Banda's regime – the Synod should have known that! Too late did it realise its fate, otherwise it should have repented to the Lord in sack cloth and ashes earlier on and probably have begun to carry out its prophetic call.

In 1992 when the churches in Malawi sensed the winds of political change blowing from Zambia, and then in Kenya, they realised that MCP politics were deteriorating in Malawi. So instead of thinking that their interests were being preserved by the status quo, they discovered that actually their interests would be preserved by going contrary to the status quo. So came the Lenten Pastoral Letter, then the churches' initiatives to form PAC; the massive support of individual pressure groups; the active participation in the multi–party campaign until the 14 June 1993 victory of multi–party politics. No its most of the ministers of the `Word' were at this time so busy preaching the best sermons against the MCP regime – digging into the grievances committed by MCP between 1964 – 1992 which otherwise would have been more meaningful to the people if they had spoken out the time these things happened.

The Church itself is aware of failing to speak out during the time it mattered. Blantyre Synod has so confessed but Livingstonia Synod feels that it was carrying out a prophetic ministry only that it was more geared towards encouragement to the oppressed rather than to the oppressor. But if it was carrying out this ministry why was it sending out loyal messages showing an unconditional support of the MCP between 1980–1990?

One wonders at whether the church has also become a political institution with politicians for prophets who practicing `dirty politics' have neither permanent enemies nor permanent friends but permanent interests which they will pursue at any cost! Of course the oppressor also needs the pastoral care of the Church but the best pastoral care she/he can receive is to help her/him see the sin of oppression and to provoke her/him into repentance – so that turning away from oppression, she/he may see God in the oppressed.

Unless Livingstonia Synod redefines its so called `prophetic' ministry, I wonder what it will do next. Now it is so `prophetic' as things change in Malawi – what about tomorrow when the new system of government takes over? What will its prophetic ministry be like – will it identify itself with the ruling regime: AFORD, UDF, MCP or whoever comes to power? Or will it deliberately take a stand for the rank and file? Will it construct a teaching that will reflect the interests of those people who do not matter in the eyes of the bourgeois but matter so much in the eyes of God? Whither prophetic ministry, Livingstonia Synod?

The history of the Church–State relationship in Malawi in particular as understood by Livingstonia Synod shows the temptation that finds expression in the favour of Constantinian and Lutheran models at the expense of the prophetic model. It is not very self evident that the church understands and let alone carries out its prophetic ministry.

Bibliography

Barkat, A.M. & Mutambirwa, J., *Challenge to the Church: The Kairos Document and Commentaries*, Geneva: WCC, 1985.

Barth, K., *Church Dogmatics*, vol II/1, Edinburgh: T & T Clark, 1957.

George, T., *Theology of the Reformers*, Nashville: Broadman Press, 1988.

Hallencreutz, C. & Moyo, A (eds) *Church and State in Zimbabwe*, Gweru: Mambo Press, 1988.

Hansen, H.B., *Mission, Church and State in a Colonial Setting Uganda 1980–1925*, London: Heinemann, 1984.

Kee, A., *Constantine Versus Christ The Triumph of Ideology*, London: SCM, 1982.

McCracken, J., *Politics and Christianity in Malawi 1875–1940: The Impact of the Livingstonia Mission in the Northern Province*, Cambridge: CUP, 1977.

Mufuka, K.N., *Mission and Politics in Malawi*, Kingston, Ontario: The Limestone Press, 1977.

Villa-Vicencio, C., *Between Christ and Caesar*, Grand Rapids: Eerdmans, 1986.

Wogaman, J.P., *Christian Perspectives on Politics*, London, SCM, 1988.

11. Malawian Poetry of the Transition: Steve Chimombo's A Referendum of the Forest Creatures and Jack Mapanje's The Chattering Wagtails of Mikuyu Prison.

Anthony J.M. Nazombe

It is by now a widely accepted fact that the dramatic social and political changes that are currently taking place in Malawi are a direct
consequence of at least two important recent events: the collapse of
Communism in the Eastern bloc countries of Europe in 1989 and the
publication early in March 1992 of the Malawian Catholic bishops'
pastoral letter, *Living Our Faith*[1]. The shift of focus among capitalist
nations from fighting Communism to building and strengthening
democracy in the world shocked their erstwhile Third World ideological allies, including the despotic Malawi Congress Party regime in
Malawi. This point was driven home when, at their meeting in Paris
in May 1992, the western donor countries decided to withhold all new
non-humanitarian aid to that Southern African country until the
political leadership had improved its human rights record, instituted
accountability and brought transparency to the business of government. For their part, the Catholic bishops strongly condemned the
political, social and economic injustice that had prevailed in Malawi
since independence, and called for immediate reforms.

Reacting to the Malawi Government's initial intransigence and lack of
cooperation, other forces of change came into play. For example,
students at the main campus of the University of Malawi, Chancellor
College in Zomba, organised a march in support of the bishops' pastoral letter, forcing the University authorities to send them to their
Easter holiday earlier than expected. On their return to the college, the
students quickly took advantage of a protest by clerical, technical and
support (CTS) staff demanding better pay, to cause further
disturbances and vandalise university property. The police had to be
called in to restore order and the college was subsequently closed

---

1 Catholic Bishops of Malawi, *Living Our Faith* (Balaka: Montfort
Missionaries, Lent 1992.)

indefinitely. Some of the students were later issued with dismissal notices.

From then on the initiative passed to workers in Blantyre and Lilongwe who, echoing the issues addressed in the pastoral letter, put down their tools and went onto the streets, demanding higher wages and better working conditions. The strikes swiftly degenerated into scenes of violence and looting and, in the ensuing battle with the police and the Malawi Young Pioneers, some forty people lost their lives. These disturbances have come to be called the May riots of 1992, a landmark in Malawi's history comparable to 3 March in 1959, the original Martyrs' Day. Through them, a new generation of political martyrs was ordained.

Another significant contribution to the pace of change was made by Chakufwa Chihana, Secretary General of the Southern African Trade Union Coordination Council (SATUCC). While attending a conference of exiled groups opposed to the Malawi Government in Lusaka, Zambia, in April 1992, Chihana publicly declared that he would return to Malawi and form a coalition of local organisations in non-violent opposition to the ruling Malawi Congress Party. On arrival at Kamuzu International Airport on 6th April, the trade union leader was arrested by the police. He was subsequently charged with three counts related to possession and importation of seditious publications, including the Catholic bishops' pastoral letter. When judgement finally came in December 1992, Chihana was sentenced to two years imprisonment with hard labour, a term later reduced by the Supreme Court of Malawi to nine months. By the time of his release in June 1993, he had become for many a living symbol of the struggle against dictatorship and human rights abuses in Malawi.

In the second half of 1992 President Banda made a number of important concessions to the advocates of change. In an address to the nation delivered on 5th July, he indicated his readiness to initiate a programme of social and political reform by creating appropriate fora at which disputes and differences could be resolved by means of discussion. In particular, he stated that ordinary Malawians could from then on meet cabinet ministers and engage them in dialogue. These were the outlines of the future Presidential Committee on Dialogue (PCD) and the Public Affairs Committee (PAC). The former would later consist of members of the cabinet while the latter would comprise representatives of the churches, the Malawi Law Society and the business community in the country.

A further significant step on the road to multiparty democracy was the arrival of the independent press, heralded by *The Malawi Financial Post*. This marked the introduction into the country of a measure of press freedom hitherto unknown. The new papers quickly went into action, courageously drawing attention to cases of human rights abuses as well as corruption in high places. In these changed circumstances, the government controlled media found themselves in the awkward position of issuing refutations every time the opposing camp made a sensational revelation or accusation.

Following closely on the heels of the independent press was the advent of pressure groups. The Alliance for Democracy (AFORD) had, since the return to Malawi of Chakufwa Chihana, been operating underground, especially in the North and in the cities and towns. In mid–September 1992, however, it was officially launched in Blantyre. Comprising former civil servants, lawyers, academics, churchmen and businessmen, the group indicated right from the beginning that its main aim was to advocate change within the framework of the constitution and the law of the country.[2] Another aim was to engage the government in a dialogue with a view to making the appropriate arrangements for a referendum in which Malawians would decide whether to retain the single party system of government or opt for a multiparty one.[3]

About a month later, another pressure group, the United Democratic Front (UDF), emerged. Consisting principally of prominent businessmen and rehabilitated politicians, the UDF was introduced as an organisation formed by 'a group of Malawians deeply concerned about the current state of the Malawi nation'[4] which would 'mount a crusade for the establishment of a genuinely democratic government in Malawi'[5]. The pressure group would, in particular, openly mobilise

---

2 Harry Chiume, then Publicity Secretary of Aford, quoted in Alaudin Osman and Jika Nkolokosa, "The Challenge on Democracy," *The Malawi Financial Post*, (October 2–15 1992), p. 16.

3 *Ibid.*, pp. 16–17.

4 Bakili Muluzi, then Interim Chairman of the UDF, quoted in Alaudin Osman, "Now, the UDF", *The Malawi Financial Post,* (16–30 October 1992), p. 13.

5 *Ibid., Ibid.*

support for a multiparty government and use peaceful and lawful means to achieve its goal of a peaceful, stable, prosperous and free society in Malawi.[6]

The formation of the UDF was announced on 19th October, just a day after President Banda had declared that a referendum would be held soon in Malawi to let the citizens decide whether they wanted a single party state or a multiparty one. This was the biggest concession made by the Malawi leader to his internal and external critics by that stage in the process of political reform.

The referendum itself is now history. As the whole world by now knows, on 14th June 1993, Malawians voted overwhelmingly in favour of a multiparty system of government. Although it strongly resisted opposition calls to resign as a result of having lost the popular mandate, the Malawi Congress Party government nevertheless agreed to the need for constitutional changes to allow for the existence of several political parties in the country. A general amnesty was declared leading to the release of all known political prisoners and enabling all citizens who went into exile to return to their country and help determine its future. The government also acceded to the establishment of two important bodies, the National Consultative Council (NCC) and the National Executive Committee (NEC), set up to supervise the transition to the first truly democratic general elections in Malawi's postcolonial history. These have since been scheduled for 17th May, 1994.

The background information given in the foregoing pages is essential to a proper appreciation of two books of poems by two of Malawi's leading poets: Steve Chimombo and Jack Mapanje.

Such a bold composition as Chimombo's *A Referendum of the Forest Creatures*[7], published and circulated inside Malawi, would have been unthinkable before the era of multiparty politics. In other words, like the independent press and the impressive amount of 'referendum verse' that it spawned, the long poem is a product of the two main factors presented at the beginning of this essay. Before the wind of

---

6 *Ibid.*, pp. 13–14.
7 S. Chimombo, *A Referendum of the Forest Creatures*, Zomba: WASI Publications, 1993. All page references are to this edition, and they appear in brackets in the text.

change heralded by the crumbling of the Berlin Wall, Chimombo, like most other authors operating from within Malawi, had to resort to a private and cryptic mode of expression in his writing in order to elude both the tough censorship laws of the country and the real possibility of political persecution.

The writer explains in his introduction that the poem was inspired by Nyakalambo, the mythical forest of animals in Kaphirintiwa in the Central Region of present day Malawi. According to Chewa oral tradition, this is the hill on which God, man and all the animals descended onto earth at the time of creation. The forest itself appears both in legend and in Steve Chimombo's earlier work, *Python! Python!*[8] as an idyllic place where all creatures lived in harmony until man committed the ritual error of making fire. As a matter of interest, this Edenic atmosphere is notable for its absence in Chimombo's latest poem.

It is a measure of Chimombo's continuing interest in oral literature and its related aesthetics that *A Referendum of the Forest Creatures* takes the form of an oral narrative. Chimombo offers it to his readers as a fable told by a folkloric figure already familiar from *Napolo Poems*[9], the Kalilombe. This is a large species of chameleon with a big proboscis. Malawians believe that when it is in labour, this animal climbs up a tree, then hurls itself onto the ground, where it bursts open and its offspring emerge from its womb. In 'Four Ways of Dying'[10], a poem which in many ways foreshadows the present one, the Kalilombe is presented as one of four 'martyrs-to-be' in a national ritual sacrifice. Where Crab, Chameleon and Mole find all kinds of excuses for not offering themselves as scapegoats, the Kalilombe readily assumes that role, hoping to effect social regeneration through its death.

As this writer has suggested elsewhere, 'Four Ways of Dying' can be read as an allegory on the role of the writer in a modern African state.[11] In this respect, the writer who takes the Kalilombe as his

---

8 S. Chimombo, *Python! Python!* Zomba: WASI Publications, 1992.

9 S. Chimombo, *Napolo Poems*, Zomba: Manchichi Publishers, 1987.

10 See S. Chimombo, *Napolo Poems*, pp.21–23.

11 See A. Nazombe, "The Role of Myth in the Poetry of Steve Chimombo", Paper presented at the Third General Conference of University Teachers of Literature and Language (ATOLL), held at the University of Botswana,

totet must be prepared to become integrated into the eternal process of spiritual renewal, one which quite often demands the supreme sacrifice. This observation is borne out by the closing paragraph of Chimombo's introduction to *A Referendum of the Forest Creatures*, where he refuses to apologise for making the Kalilombe the narrator, arguing that the animal is a perfect model of African tragedy.[12] Although it would be presumptuous to assume that the poet himself sees his role as a writer in this way, there is nevertheless evidence in the text to suggest an intimate connection between the Kalilombe and the writer himself. In the prologue, for instance, it is stated that the Kalilombe used to sing in impenetrable verbal thickets at the height of universal woe or doom, at the brink of disaster or edge of catastrophe or the advent of the floods and landslides associated with the mythical monster, Napolo. Now, however, the animal's tongue having matured, it sings more accessible songs. This account of the evolution of the Kalilombe's style also applies to the development of Chimombo's own poetic craft. Whereas at the height of political oppression in Malawi he deliberately wrote in a heavily mythical and therefore difficult mode, as the situation has improved, so too has his poetic style become increasingly narrative and ballad-like.[13]

The idea that there is a near identity between the poet and the Kalilombe is further supported by the biographical details furnished in the second stanza of the prologue. Here we are told that until recently, the Kalilombe was a chameleon in his own right, busy changing colours 'For camouflage if not survival / In the emasculation of one-party politics' (p.1). The allusion is probably to the strategy adopted by Jack Mapanje in his poetry, especially in his first book, significantly entitled *Of Chameleons and Gods*.[14] Like the Kalilombe, Chimombo stayed at home, instead of going into exile like David Rubadiri, Guy Mhone, Frank Chipasula, Felix Mnthali and now Jack Mapanje. Somehow he avoided detention and death throughout that whole period, giving rise to suspicion in some quarters of complicity with the powers that be.

Gaborone, 3–7 January, 1990, pp. 14–15.

[12] S. Chimombo, Introduction, *A Referendum of the Forest Creatures*, p. ix.

[13] See A. Nazombe (ed), *The Haunting Wind: New Poetry from Malawi*, Blantyre: Dzuka Publishing Company, 1990, p. 11.

[14] J. Mapanje, *Of Chameleons and Gods*, London: Heinemann, 1981.

A Referendum of the Forest Creatures, then, is a fable or allegory on Malawi. It is a thinly veiled account of the political, social and economic problems that precipitated the Malawi referendum of 14th June 1993. The Forest Republic in which it is set recalls Malawi's status since 1966, and such place names as Maravi, Ndirande, Dzeleka, Mwanza, Lilongwe, Sanjika and Nsanje serve to reinforce the parallel. The further revelation that Nyakalambo was divided into three regions, north, centre and south, seals the identification.

In his tale, the Kalilombe tells of how in the olden days of ancient Maravi, a mighty lion once ruled the great Nyakalambo forest with the help of a concubine and her uncle. His rule was ruthless, characterised by the detention or murder of all those who dared oppose him. The only citizens who prospered were blood relations of the lion's concubine or sycophants. Critics of the regime nevertheless continued to protest in the cryptic tongues of chameleons or in ancient prophetic mythologies. Their litany of woes included oppression and incarceration, tyranny and despotism, paranoia, nepotism, tribalism and regionalism. Eventually, the lion heard them and declared that there should be a referendum to decide whether he alone or the many should rule.

At this point, the Kalilombe interrupts the narrative to present a series of moving laments. They come from the forest's prisons, roads, rivers and ordinary citizens. We learn of the horrors of Malawi's Mikuyu, Dzeleka and Nsanje prisons through the bitter personal experiences of such animal characters as Chelule, Kadzioche, Nunkhadala, Nkhumbu and Kafadala. The torture and deprivation of prison life is complemented by carefully orchestrated accidents on the forest's roads as well as by the drownings of political opponents in its rivers and lakes. For its part, 'Lament of the Living' recalls the chorus of Canterbury women in T.S. Eliot's play, *Murder in the Cathedral*.[15] Like their counterparts in that drama, the inhabitants of Nyakalambo seem to have been 'living and partly living' during the lion's thirty year reign.

Chimombo's allegory wears quite thin as it strives to remain faithful to the sequence of events in Malawi's recent history outlined at the beginning of this paper. The Catholic bishops, for example, are

---

[15] T.S. Eliot, *Murder in the Cathedral*, London and Boston: Faber and Faber, 1968.

likened to an elephant outraged by the lion's encroachment on his preserves and rights, and scandalised by the denial of freedom of assembly and expression. The university students and the workers of Blantyre and Lilongwe appear as rhinos, hippos and buffaloes, clamouring against the depredations of the lion. The emergent independent press is also catalogued, yielding such names as *The Cicada Express*, *The Nyakalambo Star*, *The Chibori* and *The Borer*. Along with the critics and dissidents mentioned earlier on, these newspapers then launch a relentless assault on the excesses of the lion's regime.

A section entitled 'The Creatures of Multipartyism' vividly and accurately captures the verbal battles that raged between the MCP and the pressure groups in the run-up to the referendum. The irony that Chimombo skilfully exploits in his fable is that some of the insults hurled at each other by political opponents in fact smacked of the animal world. *Bongololo* (Millipede), used by the MCP to describe opposition figures as latecomers, is a case in point. As a trait, duplicity is here represented by the figure of *Mleme*, the bat, who is at home in both camps. Claiming to be born again after being recently released from prison, he initially joins the democratic forces only to revert later to the party of the lion, where he goes on to rise meteorically. He is deservedly branded traitor, opportunist, sell-out and turncoat.

The referendum itself is a very colourful and even festive occasion. The animals keen to cast their votes come from all the three regions of Nyakalambo as well as from all the major species:

> The Chinawali (sic) Tigresses, now all coy, were there.
> Walalawalala and Wakwithu went together;
> Jwangalusa did not miss out, too;
> Sodatheonse was in the forefront;
> Andilandazonse threw in his hand;
> Nkhabe brought the extreme south with him. (p.27)

If we relate this to the social reality in Malawi, the population groups represented here include bar girls or prostitutes, the country's senior citizens, the Tumbuka from the North, the Central Region Ngoni and the Yao and the Sena from the South.

The result, when it comes, corresponds closely to that recorded in the actual referendum in Malawi in 1993. The lamp, the symbol adopted by the multiparty advocates, triumphs over the black cock, the emblem of the lion's supporters. The denizens of Nyakalambo then proceed to celebrate wildly, marking the end of an era of terror and the beginning of an age of enlightenment (p.28). With the taste of victory, however, also comes the hint of self-doubt. For the first and only time becoming the collective voice of the whole society, the Kalilombe, the narrator, questions the real achievement of the referendum: 'What is dead? Is it really dead? / And what will the lamp do next?' (p.29) Towards the end of the *A Referendum of the Forest Creatures*, the writer takes us back to the main issue raised in the prologue, namely, the social role of the narrator/poet. Uneasy about the outcome of the referendum and unsure of what the future might hold for Nyakalambo, the Kalilombe retreats from the open forum to the relative safety of the *nsoro* tree, at the bottom of which the Lomwe and the Yao make offerings or oblations to the spirits of their ancestors. Curiously enough, at this point the poet/narrator reverts to the cryptic style of the earlier period; he now speaks 'in parables' and his message comes in 'bundles of riddles and proverbs' (p.29). Caution thus reasserts itself as the best means of survival. In this respect, the poet/narrator does not offer himself as the self sacrificing Kalilombe of 'Four Ways of Dying', but rather as his blood cousin, the Chameleon. The latter's main survival strategy is to pretend to go along with the nation's stated goals while retaining the liberty to criticise them in an allegorical or even more private mode. It is interesting to note, in this connection, that Steve Chimombo has not attached himself to any particular political party, unlike his now exiled colleague, Jack Mapanje, who has thrown in his lot with the United Democratic Front (UDF).

Whereas Jack Mapanje's earlier volume of verse, *Of Chameleons and Gods*, deals with the turbulent decade from 1970 to 1980, the second one, *The Chattering Wagtails of Mikuyu Prison*[16], spans the equally troubled ten year period between 1983 and 1993. The prologue with which the new collection opens establishes a clear connection between this book and the preceding one through a reference to Chingwe's Hole on Zomba Plateau. Here, however, the hole is closely identified with the detention the poet and other victims like him have experienced. Another link with *Of Chameleons and Gods* is the use of a variety of voices in these poems. The chattering wagtails of the

---

[16] J. Mapanje, *The Chattering Wagtails of Mikuyu Prison*, London: Heinemann, 1993. All pages references are to this edition and are included in the text.

book's title and the prologue, for example, are not just the birds that frequently landed in the prison yard, but also the inmates themselves and, by extension, Malawians forced by President Banda's autocratic rule to flee into exile. Also introduced in the prologue is a strongly committed stance on Jack Mapanje's part. Here is a writer who by now has obviously taken sides in the continuing political struggle in Malawi. He is among those passionately campaigning for 'Justice ' (p.1).

The poetry contained in *The Chattering Wagtails of Mikuyu Prison* discusses a wide range of issues, both private and public. What is particularly fascinating, however, is that almost all of them relate to the concerns expressed by the Catholic bishops in their pastoral latter of March, 1992, and to the demands made by such other agents of change as the university students, the workers, the independent press, the pressure groups and the western donor nations. The poem, 'Kadango Village, Even Milimbo Lagoon is Dry', for instance, records the poet's return to his place of birth only to find it drought–stricken, like other parts of the country, and the people starving. Its power derives from its vivid evocation of the devastating effect of drought on every aspect of life. The piece closes with a bitter attack on the politicians of the day for giving a false picture of the situation to the outside world, thereby blocking much needed food aid.

A composition entitled 'The Rise of the New Toadies (1983)' accurately captures the atmosphere of fear, tension and uncertainty that prevailed in Malawi after the death in a mysterious accident of four popular politicians: Messrs Aaron Gadama, Dick Matenje, Twaibu Sangala and David Chiwanga. The rumour quickly spread that the men had been killed while trying to flee the country after having been found to be implicated in some kind of plot against the government. Their badly bruised bodies were wrapped in torn prison blankets and delivered to their families by armed police, who insisted that the 'rebels' should be buried without the usual funeral rites. Malawi Congress Party youth leaguers moved from door to door, warning citizens against listening to accounts of the event given by foreign radio stations. In his poem, Mapanje, like most other observers, attributes the murder of the four politicians to a power struggle within Malawi's ruling clique between liberal and conservative elements. Unfortunately for the country, the liberals lost and the hardliners triumphed:

Apparently, the 'yobbos' only wanted the air cleared,
But the other toadies wouldn't wait; you know the pattern!
(p.10).

Throughout the first part of the collection, the writer's critical eye surveys the whole country as he persistently asks what real political, social or economic progress has been achieved since independence from Britain in 1964. Hinted at all along is the possibility that he might be straying 'out of bounds', that his frank treatment of certain subjects might offend those in power.

The section of the book called 'Chattering Wagtails' is as detailed an account as any given so far by a writer of the experience of political imprisonment. It begins on the day of the poet's arrest, with the humiliation of stripping and being thoroughly searched, and ends with the tremendous feeling of excitement on the eve of his release. 'The Streak–Tease at Mikuyu Prison, 25 September 1987' is a thorough description of the handling by warders of a newly arrived detainee which is remarkable for its grim humour. In 'Fears from Mikuyu Cells for Our Loves' attention is called to the prisoner's neighbours and colleagues as well as their fully rehearsed reactions to the arrest. They are usually the ones depended upon by the Special Branch to provide information about the detainee's movements, associates and controversial statements. In prison, Mapanje imagines what his neighbours did or said after his disappearance. Although he concludes that betrayal was the inevitable outcome, he nevertheless refuses to be bitter, remembering his experiences of a neighbour's detention eleven years before. He recalls how it was considered a crime to show any sympathy towards the 'rebel's' family.

The title poem of the whole collection, 'The Chattering Wagtails of Mikuyu Prison'; is a long account of Mapanje's induction into what a Zambian writer has described as 'the other society', that is, prison. Before he can explain the circumstances of his own arrest, the poet is given a lecture on the history of the prison. He is informed, for example, that Mikuyu Prison was named thus after fig trees as a distraction from the horror evoked by the infamous Dzeleka Prison, in Dowa District, which was opened in 1965, barely a year after Malawi's independence, to accommodate the most implacable 'rebels'. As he is being introduced to fellow inmates, the new prisoner is advised to share their wit and humour but not to be daunted by their

145

long prison terms. He is also encouraged to watch the birds, the real wagtails of Mikuyu, carefully, for they announce visitors, minister to the sick, deliver messages of cheer and foretell impending releases.

Jack Mapanje foresees his own release in 'The Delight of Aerial Signs of Release', a poem dedicated to all those who worked tirelessly to get him out of prison. The composition opens with a chilling boast made by Dr Hastings Banda following the opening of Dzeleka Maximum Security Prison: '*And there, rebels will rot, rot, rot!*' The remainder of the poem challenges that statement as the poet anticipates his own freedom. Taking the advice given by his initiators earlier on, he looks for 'aerial signs of release'. The spectacle of thousands of dragon–flies swarming over the prison yard, for example, is related to a similar event fourteen years before when two hundred political prisoners were released. On the eve of the poet's release itself, the sight of hundreds of psychedelic moths inspires the hope that more detainees will soon leave Mikuyu.

Mapanje celebrates his release from detention in a poem appropriately labelled 'The Release: Who Are You, *Imbongi*?, the centrepiece of the closing section of *The Chattering Wagtails of Mikuyu Prison*. The question in the composition's title, expressing both bewilderment and awe, comes from the Inspector General of police, whose Special Branch officers arrested the writer in the first place. Its full text reads as follows: *We've detained more distinguished people than you in this country, but we've never had the same amount of trouble as we've had over your case.* WHO ARE YOU? The trouble being referred to, of course, is the international publicity given to the poet's detention. The police are quite frankly stunned to discover that the imprisonment of a mere university lecturer could attract such embarrassing worldwide attention to the atrocities perpetrated in Malawi during the Banda era.

Jack Mapanje's reply to the Inspector General's question is cast, typically, in a folktale style; for, like Steve Chimombo, he is fascinated with oral literature:

> When the lion wrung the gazelle
> Under his smoking armpits, when
> The foaming rhinoceros pierced his
> Sharp horn or the leopard pounced;
> Did you ask, *imbongi*, who are you?
> (Even this underwear feels rough after

> Three years, seven months, sixteen
> Days and tweed jacket fungus–stinks,
> Itching like ancient goat–skins); (p.71).

The word *imbongi*, Zulu or Ngoni for praise singer, is very important here. It signifies a singer who is also free to criticise his subject. Mapanje has increasingly been adopting such a stance towards Malawi's political leadership in his poetry. The remainder of the poem under discussion recounts what actually happened on the day of the poet's release. Hand–cuffed, he was thrown into a landrover and then driven for an interview fifty miles away, presumably at the Southern Region Police Headquarters in Blantyre. During the drive, the prisoner was given no clue as to what the outcome of the interview with the Inspector General might be. His fellow prisoners' ambivalent farewell still rang in his ears:

> .... 'If this is your release,
> Then best wishes, remember you have
> Left behind fellow inmates; if further
> Charges, Mikuyu will gladly welcome
> You back; if otherwise accidentalized
> Our Gatebook signatures will testify' (p.72).

Mapanje explains in a note that the word 'accidentalize' was first used by members of the Writers' Workshop in Chancellor College, University of Malawi, in the 1983–84 academic year. Corroborating evidence comes from Steve Chimombo's *A Referendum of the Forest Creatures*. Apparently, the word means to kill and pretend it was an accident when everybody knows it was not. Obviously, Mapanje took the word with him to Mikuyu Prison in 1987 and popularised it there. Its specific frame of reference, needless to explain, was the gruesome political murder in May 1983 of Messrs Gadama, Matenje, Sangala and Chiwanga.

As he is being driven to Blantyre, then, the writer briefly considers the possibility that he, like those four politicians almost exactly eight years before, might be heading for an extrajudicial execution rather than a proper release. Mapanje's fear for his own safety was real; for, according to one story, the May 1983 victims were 'released' from Mikuyu Prison after spending a night there. However, the Special Branch officers who came to collect them were not particularly keen to leave their signatures in the appropriate gatebook, as was the usual practice.

To console himself, the poet returns to the world of the folktale, comparing himself to a mere *maccah*, a burr that will tenaciously stick to one's clothes when one is walking in the grass or to the brown ant that once crept into the elephant's ear, forcing it to scratch and scratch until the huge animal finally destroyed itself. In other words, the poet humbly projects himself as, at best, an irritant, and not as important a threat to the status quo as those murdered politicians might have been. Nevertheless, the more aggressive overtones of the insect parallel are not entirely lost on the reader. It would seem that like the Chameleon in Steve Chimombo's poem, 'Four Ways of Dying', Mapanje the poet will from now on use cunning to hasten the destruction of the present tyrannical order.

As Mary McCarthy has rightly pointed out, exiles are great readers of newspapers and collectors of clippings on events at home.[17] The fact that the press of their country is often censored makes them hungry for scraps of rumour and information which they can piece together.[18] This tendency is evident in poems written by Mapanje after his departure from Malawi in October 1991. 'Where Dissent is Meat for Crocodiles', for example, is a poem marking Martyrs' Day in Malawi which echoes a threat issued in public to his exiled political opponents by President Banda. In this reflective piece Mapanje traces Malawi's political problems to the Cabinet Crisis which shook the country soon after independence in 1964. Several ministers rebelled against Banda's autocratic style of leadership and subsequently fled the country to organise opposition from abroad. Since then, Mapanje asserts, the Malawian leader has maintained himself in power through the brutal suppression of all dissenting voices. The poet cites as recent examples of this the ruthless way in which the students' riots and workers' strikes of 1992 were handled. He also calls attention to the death in police custody of a Mangochi businessman who dared protest at the manhandling of women found wearing trousers at a Yao circumcision ceremony for boys. To Mapanje, such 'brethren in dissent' deserve to be called martyrs.

Having opened his second collection of verse with a prologue, Jack Mapanje closes it with a composition corresponding to an epilogue.

---

[17] M. McCarthy, "Exiles, Expatriates and International Emigres", *The Listener*, 86, 2226, (25 November 1971), p. 706.
[18] Ibid., Ibid.

This is 'The Deluge After Our Gweru Prison Dreams'. In a note placed between the title and the text, the poet reveals that the piece was inspired by the students' and workers' riots of 1992. He also describes the poem as 'a history of the nation', dedicated to fellow countryman, David Rubadiri, who has been living in exile since the Cabinet Crisis of 1964. Rubadiri was at the time Malawi's ambassador to the United States of America and to the United Nations. He now lives in Botswana, where he is Professor of Education at the local university.

True to its declared purpose, the poem is a detailed account of the fate that has befallen the dreams of Malawi's development which Dr. Banda claims that he had in Gweru Prison, Southern Rhodesia, when he was a political prisoner there between 3 March 1959 and 1 April 1960, during the State of Emergency in Nyasaland. The dreams in question refer to the following specific projects: the removal of Malawi's capital from Zomba in the South to Lilongwe in the Centre; the construction of a highway all along Lake Malawi's shore and the establishment of a national university in Zomba.

In the first part of the piece the poet shows how most of these dreams have by the early nineties finally unravelled. The idea of a new capital, for instance, in many ways still remains unfulfilled because the country's economy has been undermined by persistent droughts, making it difficult for the government to set aside enough funds for the completion of the project. Secondly, the section of the Lakeshore Road that was actually constructed has now been reduced to 'crustaceous tarmac' and 'yawning potholes' that cripple even the hardiest of vehicles. Thirdly, the local university students, hitherto well known for their docility, now dare take the institution to court for unlawful dismissal, supported by none other than the Head of the Law Department himself, who then proceeds to defend Chakufwa Chihana against sedition charges.

The second part of the poem places developments on the Malawian political scene in both a global and a regional context. The poet argues that the democratisation process in his country benefited greatly from the change in international relations which followed the disintegration of the Eastern bloc as well as from western donor countries' insistence on linking aid packages with political reforms, especially transparency and good governance.

Right from the beginning, Banda was prepared to, in his own words, 'sup with the devil himself' in order to fulfil his Gweru dreams. Thus, when, in 1965, he failed to attract funding from Britain or any of the other regular donors for his plan to move the country's capital from Zomba to Lilongwe, he quite unexpectedly turned to apartheid South Africa for help. By August 1966, he had announced that Malawi might seek South African expertise in the design of the new capital.[19] In March 1967, formal contacts began with a visit to South Africa by a Malawian ministerial delegation which resulted in the signing of a new trade agreement between the two countries.[20] On 12 December 1967, diplomatic relations were established between Malawi and South Africa, leading to Malawi's alienation from other members of the Organisation of African Unity (OAU). In March 1968, South Africa announced that it was setting up a Loans Fund for the Promotion of Economic Cooperation, 'to grant direct assistance....to well disposed developing countries – particularly in Africa.'[21] The first loan to be made from the Fund would be R8 million to Malawi, for the first phase of the construction of the new capital.[22]

Jack Mapanje picks up the point about Malawi's strange relationship with South Africa in his poem, suggesting that the major western donors having withdrawn aid from Malawi, President Banda might once again seek assistance from South Africa. Unfortunately for the Malawi leader, however, even South Africa itself has been profoundly affected by the 'happy debris of the Berlin Wall'. The process of reform is evident from the unbanning and/or legalisation in early 1990 of such organisations as the African National Congress, the Pan African Congress, the South African Communist Party and the United Democratic Front, as well as the unconditional release from prison of Nelson Mandela. According to Mapanje, it is doubtful whether after all these changes and in view of its own internal problems, South Africa will still want to extend its generosity to the present regime in Malawi.

19 See P. Short, *Banda*, London and Boston: Routledge and Kegan Paul, 1974, p. 290.
20 Ibid., p. 296.
21 Ibid., p. 305.
22 Ibid., Ibid.

The third section of 'The Deluge After Our Gweru Dreams' begins with the poet's approval of the timely action taken by the youths and the workers of Malawi. It then challenges the government of the day to name any dissident, living or dead, internal or exiled, who might be behind the strikes, demonstrations and riots. Masauko Chipembere, Jomo Chikwakwa, the Chisiza brothers, Silombera, Kanada, are all exonerated, as are the more recent 'rebels': Aaron Gadama, Dick Matenje, Twaibu Sangala and David Chiwanga.

The fourth and final part of the poem criticises Malawians for their gullibility throughout the period of single party rule and goes on to debunk all prison dreams, including those of the addressee, David Rubadiri, in H.M. Prison Khami, Bulawayo, in 1959, and those of the speaker and his fellow wagtails in Mikuyu Prison. As in *Of Chameleons and Gods*, so too here, Mapanje expresses his total distrust of all 'lie-achieved' worlds.

Apart from being a history of Malawi, the poem was obviously also intended to be an epitaph on the Banda era. However, as a realist, Mapanje does not foresee an entirely smooth transition to the new multiparty dispensation. Instead, he squarely confronts the possibility of chaos in the wake of President Banda's departure. Hence the last two couplets, characteristically rendered as a rhetorical question:

> ... Whatever, the question still
> Lingers: won't toxic mushrooms burgeon
> Under those rotten logs of nightmares
> That now threaten *après moi, le deluge*? (p. 98)

The toxic mushrooms suggest destruction on the scale of Hiroshima and Nagasaki at the close of the Second World War, whereas the French allusion is to President Charles de Gaulle's apocalyptic prophecy that after him, France would be plunged into political, social and economic instability. Is this, perhaps, the fate that awaits Malawi after Banda?

From the above discussion of Jack Mapanje's *The Chattering Wagtails of Mikuyu Prison*, it should be abundantly clear that his latest poetry speaks to a society undergoing momentous change. Like the Catholic bishops' pastoral letter, the students' and workers' riots of May 1992, as well as the efforts of the independent press and the opposition parties, it calls attention to persistent poverty, social inequality, inadequate health services, harsh censorship laws and the flouting of basic human rights in Malawi. From that point of view, it also covers much the same thematic terrain as Steve Chimombo's *A Referendum of the Forest Creatures*. However, the similarity must end there; for, unlike Chimombo, who has signalled a withdrawal from the public forum after the referendum, the exiled Mapanje continues to be a close observer of events back home, identifying problems in the movement towards multiparty democracy and earnestly trying to find solutions to them. Not contented with mere poetic commentary, the writer has recently aligned himself with the United Democratic Front (UDF). Thus by courageously assuming the role of the Ngoni *imbongi*, at once eulogiser and critic, Mapanje stands poised to make a more substantial contribution to the process of political reform in Malawi than does his home based counterpart, who has chosen to retreat into the private world of parables and riddles after an all too brief foray into his country's public life.

12. The "Smaller" Churches and Big Government

Klaus Fiedler

1. The Three–fold Face of Christianity in Africa

When Christianity came to Sub–Saharan Africa, it was far from being a monolithic bloc. While there was much cooperation among the various Protestant missions,[1] Catholics and Protestants were more competitors than colleagues.[2] Since the second half of the last century many African Instituted Churches have sprung up. In the beginning they were often seen as "hardly Christian", but since the 1950s they have increasingly been accepted as genuine Christian churches. This threefold face of Christianity in Africa is the major organizing principle of Adrian Hastings' *History of African Christianity*. He divides African Christianity into three groups: Protestant mission churches, Catholic mission churches and Independent churches.[3] Against Hastings I contend that the church in Africa has at least a fourfold face. It is not good enough to lump all Protestants together, because in doing so the "bigger" churches are usually taken to stand for the lot.

This other group among the Protestants goes by various names, and is in most countries the smaller group. Since small is – at least sometimes – beautiful, and since it is the researcher's task to come as

---

[1] This was often expressed in "comity agreements", informal or formal arrangements that would allot a certain territory exclusively – as far as Protestants were concerned – to one mission, so that there would be no competition. The Africans were supposed "to be saved from the historical divisions of European Christianity which mean nothing to them" and the missionaries from competition. Such comity agreements were countrywide in Zaire e.g., but in Malawi only existed between the three Presbyterian/Reformed missions. Anglicans and Evangelicals did not accept these imposed borders.

[2] The Roman Catholic Church never accepted comity agreements, unless imposed by government.

[3] Adrian Hastings, *A History of African Christianity 1950 – 1975*, Cambridge et al.: CUP, 1986 (1979), 2.

close to reality as possible, I have, for several years, concentrated on these churches in Africa, which sometimes here in Malawi are collectively called "the smaller churches". Size is not necessarily a permanent criterion, but origins might be. Therefore, I have tried to describe the fourth face of Christianity in Africa by its distinct origins.

All Protestant missionary activity in Africa originated in revivals of religion in the West. The most important of them was the "Great Awakening", which began in 1734 and which became a major missionary force by 1792.[4] Because these missions played the greatest role in changing the religious landscape of Africa (and beyond) I have called them the "classical missions". The classical Protestant churches are represented in Malawi by the CCAP (originating from three Presbyterian and Reformed missions) and by the Anglican Church. The majority of the Catholic missions in Africa come from a Catholic Revival parallel to the Great Awakening, so I include them into the group of "classical missions/churches". Reliable statistics are hard to come by, but the classical churches may comprise about 70% of all Christians in Malawi, the remaining 30% being divided between the African Instituted Churches and what I call the post–classical churches.

The post–classical churches all originated in later revivals, the Restorationist Revival of the 1830s, the Holiness Revival of 1859/1873, the Pentecostal Revival of 1906 and the Charismatic Revival of the 1960s.[5] Their differences cannot be seen only in their different historical origins, but also in attitudes and relationships. The post–classical churches are in their homelands minority churches, whereas the classical churches are usually the "national church". The post–classical churches insist on separation of church and state, the classical churches gladly accept various forms of "establishment", if

---

[4] 1792 was marked by the publication of William Carey's *An Enquiry into the Obligation of Christians to Use Means for the Conversion of the Heathen*, Leicester 1792, and by the founding of the Baptist Missionary Society (then: Particular Baptist Society for Propagating the Gospel among the Heathen). 1792 is usually taken as the year that ushered in the "Great Century" of Missions (K.S. Latourette) 1792–1914.

[5] Among the post–classical churches in Malawi I include those churches which in other parts of Africa are classical churches, but which follow in Malawi a post–classical pattern (like Baptists, Lutherans and Moravians).

A Historical Typology of Missions and Churches

Revival	Date	Emphasis	Denominations	Missions	In Malawi
Reformation	1517/22	Scripture alone, faith alone, grace alone	Lutherans, Reformed/Presbyterians, Anglicans	None	None
The pre-classical missions					
Puritanism/ Pietism	1581/1675	Personal Conversion and practical Christianity	Congregationalists, Baptists, Moravians (Herrnhut)	Few missions: Congregationalists, Moravians	None
The classical missions and churches					
Great Awakening	1734 (1792)	Personal conversion and practical Christianity. Post-millennial eschatology	Created the missionary vision of the Reformation ("classical") denominations. Methodists	The Great Missionary Revival (the classical missions): BMS 1792; LMS 1795; CMS 1799 and many others	UMCA (Anglican) 1861; Free Church of Scotland Mission (Livingstonia) 1875; Church of Scotland Mission (Blantyre) 1876; Dutch Reformed Church Mission (Nkhoma) 1889 [CCAP]

155

Post-classical Missions

Restorationist Revival	1830s	Restoration of NT Christianity. Pre-millennial eschatology. Strong ecclesiastical emphasis.	Christian Brethren; Churches of Christ; Apostolic Churches; Seventh Day Adventists; (Jehovah's Witnesses)	All the new denominations developed missionary work not long after being founded	Seventh Day Adventists (1893/1902); Church(es) of Christ (1906); Jehovah's Witnesses/Watchtower (1909/37); New Apostolic Church (1923)
Holiness Revival	1859/73	Conversion, sanctification, pre-millennial eschatology	Free Methodists, Church of the Nazarene, Salvation Army	interdenominational faith missions (1865); some denominational missions	Zambezi Industrial Mission (1892); Nyassa Industrial Mission (1893); South Africa General Mission (1895); Holiness denominations (Church of the Nazarene, Salvation Army, Free Methodists, after 1957)
Pentecostal Revival	1906	Full Gospel, charismatic gifts	Assemblies of God and other Pentecostal or Apostolic Churches	Developed soon a strong missionary movement (denominational)	Assemblies of God (1930); Pentecostal Holiness Association (1932); Apostolic Faith Mission (1932); others after 1945
Charismatic Revival	1960s	Similar to Pentecostal Revival	Revival mainly within the classical ("mainline") denominations	Missionary movement only developing	Living Waters Church, Agape Life Church and others

available. Finally, the post–classical churches see human society usually in a less positive light than the classical churches do.

Here and elsewhere I argue that these churches are different enough to warrant separate study,[6] and this paper attempts to pursue this aim in relation to the process of political change that started in Malawi with the publication of the Lenten Pastoral Letter of the Catholic Bishops on 8 March 1992.

2. General Perceptions

Though the post–classical churches are rarely clearly defined, there are some quite widespread perceptions as to their peculiarities. I summarize and list some of them here:

1. They are conservative – therefore they support the status quo.
2. They keep out of politics – therefore they have no prophetic voice.
3. They are after individual salvation only – therefore they are not interested in the improvement of society.
4. They are chiefly interested in the hereafter – therefore they support the powers that be as long as they are in this world.

This basically negative picture, logical as it may look, does not necessarily match reality, and in this paper I want to check it against reality in Malawi, concentrating on one issue (political involvement) and on one point in time (the Pastoral Letter and its consequences).[7]

---

6 First put forward for missions in: Klaus Fiedler, *Ganz auf Vertrauen. Geschichte und Kirchenverständnis der Glaubensmissionen*, Gießen/Basel: Brunnen, 1992, 12–35. To be published as *The History of the Faith Missions* by Regnum, Oxford, 1994.

7 As archival material is not yet accessible, I have to rely on limited and uneven material, in which oral sources and newspapers play a major role.

3. Limitations to Post–classical Participation in Politics

The post–classical churches are quite varied, but some generalizations may be attempted.

1. The post–classical churches are usually small. Therefore their chance to influence political processes is small, too. What influence can a denomination like the Free Methodists with about 7000 communicant members, spread over all the three regions of Malawi, effectively exert?[8]

2. Many of the post–classical churches have congregationalist structures of church government, like the Baptists and, much more strictly, the Churches of Christ. For the Churches of Christ there just *is* no higher authority than the local congregation, and even though the Baptists, while insisting on local church autonomy, do have a national "convention", this is a comparatively weak structure, with very limited possibilities of the leadership speaking for the church.[9] In Baptist churches political involvement therefore is most likely to take not corporate but individual forms, with the local congregation's support deciding if an individual political initiative can be seen as "just personal" or as "Baptist".

3. Some of the post–classical churches, for theological reasons, do not join interdenominational organizations like the Christian Council of Malawi. Therefore they have not shared in the CCM's political witness, which the government may have taken as support for its policies. Here again the Seventh Day Adventists are the most important case,[10] but neither do the Pentecostal and Charismatic churches belong to the Christian Council.

---

[8] That this is already different with the Seventh Day Adventists with about 150000 full members (and growing fast) is shown by the MCP's attempts to woo them in 1993.

[9] The Executive Committee can make statements *as the* Executive Committee, but "resolutions or statements are non-binding".

[10] There would be some reason to include the Jehovah's Witnesses here as even more extreme among the post-classical churches. Their political involvement (and consequent immense suffering) was caused by their strict policy not to involve themselves in politics (not even by buying [one-] party cards). The Jehovah's Witnesses could be included under post-classical churches because they *probably* had their early roots in the same

4. Churches with a very strong doctrine of separation of state and church are usually not keen on *publicly* commenting on political and social issues. They are also most likely not to have sister churches abroad who would do this for them, like the Church of Scotland did for the CCAP in 1992.

4. Post-classical Political Involvement through the Christian Council of Malawi

On 8 March 1992 the Pastoral Letter was read in all Catholic parishes, in June the CCAP and the World Alliance of Reformed Churches Commission had demanded that the government institutionalize dialogue, and when nothing seemed to happen, in August 1992 the CCM wrote to the President demanding a referendum and criticizing some abuses of power. For the standards of that time this was a very strong action, lining up most Protestant denominations behind the Catholics. This letter was signed by all member churches of the CCM, classical and post-classical alike. The post-classical signatories were: Baptist Convention of Malawi; Evangelical Lutheran Church; Zambezi Evangelical Church; Free Methodist Church; African Methodist Episcopal Church; Providence Industrial Mission (= African Baptist Assemblies). Later one of the two signatories from the (classical) Nkhoma Synod withdrew his signature with apologies to the Ngwazi,[11] but none of the post-classical representatives did. Neither did the post-classical churches outside the CCM express any support for the one-party state. The post-classical member churches of the CCM also signed the November 1992 letter to the President, demanding that fairness be applied to the referendum process, that all harassment should be stopped and that all prisoners of conscience be

Restorationist Revival (1830s) as the Seventh Day Adventists, the Churches of Christ, the Christian Brethren and Apostolic Church (Irvingites). But the Jehovah's Witnesses on their side do not have fellowship with any of the post-classical churches, and these in turn consider them as "sects" or as "marginal". This (Pmar) is also the classification which David Barrett uses for them in the *World Christian Encyclopedia*.

11 The signature of the official representative of Nkhoma Synod was never withdrawn, but the withdrawal of the one signature seems to have been accepted by *all* parties as representing the real attitude of the Synod, which was therefore suspended from the CCM.

released.[12] The leadership of these churches in general supported the CCM political stance.[13] This I was personally able to witness when I had the privilege of attending a CCM Heads of Churches meeting in Blantyre,[14] where classical and post–classical Heads of Churches alike simply did not call the Life President "Life President", and where tone and content of their discussion showed an equally refreshing lack of deference to political authority.

After this view from the CCM perspective I would like to draw attention to individual churches for which I have some detailed material.

5. The Baptist Convention of Malawi

True to their customary attitude, the Baptists did not issue a public statement of any kind. But their democratic form of church government was seen in a new light as soon as the changes began:

> In fact in the old system Baptists were out of place since democracy is the form of church government that has been identified with our heritage".[15]

That they were out of place in the old system had been shown to some Baptists at least quite clearly before the Pastoral Letter. In two cases of internal dissent which involved property[16] or position[17] the

---

[12] The Christian Council of Malawi – The Life President Ngwazi Dr. H. Kamuzu Banda, 4.11.1992.

[13] Explicitly stated in Int Rev Chipuliko, Providence Industrial Mission, 8.1993.

[14] All agreed that it was a law made and now to be repealed by the MCP, not a law to be repealed due to the process of transition to democracy. For a different opinion of the relationship of the dress code to the process of political change see Introduction p. 11.

[15] The Baptist Convention of Malawi 1993 Annual Report, 1.

[16] A congregation not very far from Blantyre wanting to leave the Baptist Convention and join another denomination (no problem about that), but also wanting to take the church building with them, which was the property of the Baptist Convention.

[17] In Zomba Pastor Gama fell foul with his congregation in 1992. He was also under discipline of the convention for having squandered funds as General Secretary.

"defeated" group appealed to the MCP for help, which duly accepted the privilege of offering that help. In Zomba the party chairman acted highhandedly and violently against the congregation, and in Blantyre the chairman and vice–chairman of the local association[18] and the general secretary of the Baptist Convention were summoned to the MCP office for correction. When they refused to accept MCP guidance, they were threatened that the church building would be turned into a CCAM office. One of the participants is still today convinced that only the Pastoral Letter, which came out a few days after this "educational conference", saved them from further trouble.[19]

The issue of his attitude to a dictatorial government became very personal for Rev Akim Chirwa, pastor of Soche Baptist Church in Blantyre, when he heard from a friend that the Aford pressure group was to be founded but that the founders were in need of a place for the inaugural meeting the police would not immediately think of. Hearing this, he offered Soche Baptist Church, and so the meeting took place in the small room on the left side of the sanctuary, while in the other small room on the right side Mrs Martha Chirwa, Mrs Chiume and Wambali Mkandawire prayed for its success.[20] At the end even a group photo was made on the steps leading into the church.[21]

The Chirwa's had received their theological training at the Baptist Seminary in Gweru, Zimbabwe, where they also studied Liberation Theology, Black Theology and African Theology. There Rev Chirwa understood that sin is not only personal and individual, but that there is also structural sin. Therefore the church had to concern itself with these sins, too, like injustice and oppression.

---

18 In the Baptist tradition a number of local congregation form an association. The association furthers fellowship and mutual assistance, but has no governing authority.
19 Int Rev Akim Chirwa 7.3.1994.
20 It was not so difficult to maintain secrecy. Rev and Mrs Chirwa asked no one from the church committee for permission, and to all people around it looked like a normal Saturday morning church activity. It could have been a wedding, or, if one would miss the bride at that, it could easily have been a retreat with people coming from other places even in cars.
21 Was this another way of camouflaging?

Rev Chirwa did not and does not understand himself as a politician.[22] As a pastor he wants to keep out of party politics, but he and his wife felt that they had to support for theological reasons a political pressure group fighting for an end to oppression.[23] In addition he wanted to help achieve religious freedom, especially the freedom of the pulpit.[24]

When the Chirwas had to make this decision, they could not inform their church committee. But as Rev Chirwa preached every Sunday, sermons on "political" issues not being excluded, and as the Chirwa's made their stand clear, the leadership of the congregation supported them. In this way, for a certain time, their house became a nerve centre for the exchange of "seditious" information[25] and for counselling those who struggled. When the possession of seditious literature or the access to seditious fax machines and photocopiers landed many in such renowed places as Chichiri Prison, not too far from Soche Baptist Church, the Chirwas helped with prayer, advice and practical assistance, including bringing those who suffered into touch with Red Cross and Legal Aid.

In my opinion, the Chirwas' attitude can be seen as a typical Baptist attitude. It is not the leadership on the national level which is supposed to act, but individuals, committed to their faith based on the whole biblical message, who are willing, for the sake of their faith, to take up a minority position. But though doing this alone, their congregation would endorse their step, and even share in the implementation. All this would happen initially through informal decision making processes.

The Soche Baptist case, though typically Baptist, does not represent the attitude of all Baptists. The Chirwas reported that those members of their congregation who had less education would also usually be

---

22 This in turn did not exclude his joining Aford as a member and selling membership cards when it was still "seditious" to do so (Rendell Day, 12.3.1994).

23 Int Martha and Akim Chirwa 7.3.1994.

24 "Contrary to the claims of the MCP government, we had no religious freedom. We were not allowed to preach the biblical message on peace and justice" (bid.).

25 For example a local church leader would come to the pastor, saying: "I found some information which might be of interest to you".

less active in their support for Christian political action, and would be more willing to go along with the status quo.

It would need much research to find out how Baptists outside the cities reacted to the changing political climate. From the limited amount of information available to me, the case of the remote Sambaimfa Baptist Congregation (not far from Mayaka) seems to be typical. They were not in any way actively involved in the process of bringing about change, but they were informed at least in general, and they clearly went along with it. They were also aware that Emmanuel Chinkwita was the chairman of their denomination,[26] and they were aware of his political activities, too. If observations like these can be generalized to some extent, this would not make the grassroot Baptists to be leaders in the transition process, but neither would it make them a force for the willing support of loyalty, obedience, discipline and dictatorship.[27]

Within the Baptist Convention the [American Southern Baptist] missionary influence is still strong.[28] The majority of the missionaries, especially those living in the Central Region, seem to have been not too unhappy with the Ngwazi's version of religious freedom,[29] and

---

[26] This knowledge of the denominational chairman is not regular, for example, among Baptists in Germany.

[27] Based on conversations of Rendell Day and Klaus Fiedler with the leaders of the church in February 1994.

[28] The work of the Baptist Convention of Malawi originates in Southern Baptist missionary activities starting in 1954, with the first resident missionaries and the first congregation in 1960 (Rendell Day, From Gowa Industrial Mission to Landmark Missionary Baptists: one Hundred Years of Baptist Churches in Malawi. Public Seminar Paper, Department of Theology and Religious Studies, 17.3.1994, p. 14.).

[29] Vividly portrayed on a full first page in the propaganda paper "Guardian Today" of 12.-18.5.1993. The article starts: "For all practical purposes, we have freedom of worship in Malawi", and it supports this claim by sporting a picture of 1978 where the Ngwazi shakes hands with Archbishop James Chiona. The caption starts: "His Excellency the Life President is a man who does not interfere with freedom of worship in this country." Then: "... during the national services of worship ... he brings together Protestants, Catholics, Moslems, Sikhs and Hindus to worship together." The Jehovah's Witnesses are not mentioned, however.

some definitely feared change as it would bring disorder.[30] But others supported the process of change right from the beginning.[31]

The Chirwas were not alone in their support for change. Akim Chirwa was able to share his attitudes with Fletcher Kaiya, the Baptist Convention's General Secretary, who also strongly supported the changes. He saw the Banda regime as usurpation, and he expressed this by telling the people of MBC[32] that the President must not be called *Namalenga* (Creator), as that title was reserved for God alone.[33]

The most visible Baptist contribution to the process of change were the activities of Rev Emmanuel Chinkwita Phiri, pastor of Lilongwe Baptist Church[34] and Chairman of the Baptist Convention. He worked for change as Acting General Secretary of the CCM for a short time, and as Acting Chairman of the Public Affairs Committee during the period of its peak activity leading up to the referendum.[35] There were probably two attempts to poison him and one to kill him in a car accident.[36] In addition he and his wife Jane were harassed at the road bloc at Kamuzu Barrage and threatened with death.[37]

---

30 Mrs Chirwa was able to comfort some of them, telling them that these pressure groups wanted democracy, not disorder (Int. 7.3.1994).

31 For example Teresa and Rendell Day of Zomba. Teresa Day, together with women leaders from various Baptist congregations in the area, conducted pre-referendum voters' education using the Roman Catholic bishops' pastoral letter *Choosing Our Future* (2.2.1993). A sideline note: I was surprised to learn that even this second pastoral letter had to be transported from the printing press at Balaka with the same secrecy as the first letter.

32 Fletcher Kaiya works in the Baptist Media Centre in Blantyre and is also a radio programmer. His position as Baptist Convention General Secretary is spare time.

33 Information from Rendell Day, end of 1992.

34 He received his advanced training at the Baptist Seminaries at Arusha (Tanzania) and Rüschlikon (Switzerland).

35 "As we meet for our Annual General Meeting we are proud and thankful to God that during the course of these dramatic changes, we have not been spectators at all. We have stood our ground on what we believe ... The role that our chairman played as Chairman of PAC was quite significant" (The Baptist Convention of Malawi 1993 Annual Report, 1).

36 Unattributable interview. See also: "The Referendum in Malawi: Free Expression Denied", *Article 19: Censorship News*, Issue 22, April 1993, 8f.

37 Personal communication ("I was ready to die") and Patrick Kalagho, "I was harassed, says Chinkwita" in *The Nation*, 25.10.1993. The MCP paper *Malawi*

What Chinkwita did, he did as an individual, not under instructions from the Baptist Convention. But though there were some questions, the Convention, when it met, supported him as its Chairman.[38] But because of the Baptist understanding of congregational church government, the support from his congregation may be more relevant. In his congregation also there were and are members unhappy with his position, but the congregation supported him in what he did.[39]

In his Christian attitude Chinkwita differs from Chirwa in one important point: Chirwa did not accept any position in any party, he wants to remain non-partisan for the sake of his ministry. Chinkwita, to the contrary, joined UDF, and accepted a position in its leadership. This meant that he would no longer be Acting Chairman of the recently revived Public Affairs Committee, where he was replaced by Dr. Silas Ncozana of Blantyre Synod. But he can still remain a pastor of his congregation and Chairman of the Baptist Convention.

I close this section with two episodes, one from the educated Baptist membership and one from the Baptist fringe. In the aftermath of the drought the Baptist Mission (together with other missions and churches) was heavily involved in food aid in the Zomba area. One day, when maize was to be distributed in Mposa in Machinga District in a drought relief project in 1991, the chief stood up and thanked the Ngwazi for bringing the maize, but a local Baptist pastor replied: "No, the *Baptists* are the ones bringing us the maize". The other episode, later in the process of change, well after the referendum. I was at-

---

News afterwards tried to create the impression that Chinkwita had provoked the guard (Reader's letter by Augustine Chilumpha Banda, Lilongwe, titled [over four columns]: "Why did Chinkwita fail to answer the question?" (*Malawi News*, 13–19.11.1993).

38 The Baptist Convention will elect a new Chairman later this year. According to the constitution, Chinkwita can not be reelected.

39 In discussions during the Faith and Knowledge Seminar no. 32, 17 March 1994, (Rendell Day, The Case for the Separation of State and Church) there was consensus that this put him in a different category from the other two "political Reverends" Aaron Longwe and Peter Kaleso. They had left the congregational ministry for specialized activities, and their Synod did not endorse them fully, whereas Chinkwita remained an active congregational pastor. (He stressed this point incidentally when he visited me during the lunch break when Parliament met to repeal the dress code and a few other oppressive laws. He related that he had just conducted a wedding and that some people there were astonished to see him as an ordinary pastor.)

tending a Baptist Sunday morning service, the preacher was a school teacher. She preached about repentance, and she started her sermon by showing the power of repentance and salvation: "Even His Excellency, if he would repent, could still find salvation, and even John Tembo." I have included these two episodes here as evidence for grassroot participation in the process of change.

6. The Seventh Day Adventist Church

The Seventh Day Adventists are a special case among the evangelical churches in Malawi. They are a well organized international Protestant church. They have a strongly evangelical piety, but a distinct theology, which stresses eschatology and the strict separation between state and church and keeps them a bit apart from other evangelical churches, so that for example they do not belong to the Christian Council.[40]

Their theology of separation of state and church makes them reluctant to make public statements on "political" issues.[41] But that is no sign of support for an authoritarian political system trying to control all aspects of life.[42] To the contrary, this attitude is a clear rebuff of a government usurping religious qualities.[43] That the Ngwazi once turned to the SDA to attend prayers at Malamulo was not a sign of

---

[40] For an insightful book on the history of the Seventh Day Adventist Church see: R.W. Schwarz, *Light Bearers to the Remnant*, Mountain View/Oshawa: Pacific Press, 1979.

[41] "We teach and advise our members and believers that if they desire to vote, to do so according to the dictates of their own individual consciences enlightened by a due regard for sanctified Christian principles" (SDA Director Pastor Masoka interviewed in *The New Express* 11th–17th June [the referendum issue]).

[42] "Our refusal to take part in party politics is not a lack of sympathy with the attainment of proper government, but it is due to following the counsel of Christ that His 'Kingdom is not of this world'" (*ibid.*).

[43] The situation is becoming more complicated now, because the newly appointed MCP Secretary General testifies to a clear conversion through a SDA preacher while serving 13 of 22 years imprisonment: "Since I was baptized in prison on January 26, 1992 all the hatred for my enemies [MCP] was buried in the water of baptism" (*The New Voice* 11.–17.10.1993 quoting Gwanda Chakuamba in the article: Kalera Mhango: "Did Tembo bribe Gwanda with K10m?")

SDA support (why should they refuse someone who wants to pray ...), but of his desperation to claim some religious support beyond that from parts of Nkhoma Synod.[44] The SDA Church in this connection made it clear that there was nothing wrong in accepting a donation to help with the renovation of the church and that neither this nor any other present would buy them.

At this time accusations were rife that the SDA Church was support-ing the MCP. Was the newly acquired MCP leader Gwanda Cha-kwamba not a Seventh Day Adventist? Did he not claim to have read through the whole Bible many times while in prison?[45] In addition, one of the newly appointed ministers, Ziyenda, was also a Seventh Day Adventist. The MCP press made him a Reverend, and so did MCP leaders in Parliament.[46] But again in the free press it was quickly pointed out that Ziyenda had been a SDA pastor, but was no longer.[47] After this in the MCP press also his title was changed from Hon. Rev. Ziyenda to the simple Hon. Ziyenda.[48] It was also easy to observe that Chakuamba, who made some references to his SDA conversion very early after his "defection" from UDF, soon stopped to allude to things like that.

The Seventh Day Adventist Church even went out of her way to pub-lish a weighty document on her position in the process of change. The church made it clear that its apolitical stance does not mean support for oppression, and that it would in no way exclude the search for a

---

44 He made a similar attempt to claim Catholic support with this year's martyrs' prayers, which he attended at St. Montfort Church in Blantyre. By his absence Archbishop Chiona made it clear that Dr Banda had come to pray and not for politics, so he was received by the local parish priest, Monsignor Lawrence Simbota. The *Daily Times* (by some post-classical church leaders fondly called "Daily Lies", by others "Daily Noise") saw things differently, claiming that "he led the nation in prayer" (7.3.1994). The parish council announced through MBC that all regular Sunday activities would proceed as usual.

45 Maundu Mwale of Lilongwe challenged his conversion in the *Nation* of 22 October 1993 with a letter titled "Born again indeed".

46 "Our Reverend" (Hansard).

47 Seventh Day Adventists do not use the title "Reverend", but call their ministers "Pastor".

48 Ziyenda failed to be nominated in his constituency as a candidate for the general elections (*Daily Times*, 22.3.1994).

better society. "We did not write the Pastoral letter, but we fully support it."[49]

The document pointed out that there had been SDA resistance, especially from the side of women who refused to dance for the President, especially on a Sabbath. This was also made clear in a reader's letter.

> I have heard from many people that the Seventh Day Adventist Church in Malawi is for the Malawi Congress Party. This belief seems to be strengthened by the District Party Chairman for Blantyre, Charles Kamphalusa.
> A point of order please: MCP leaders know the stand of our church. As a member of the Seventh Day Adventist Church, I would like to educate the nation that there is no moment that the ruling party has loved this church.
> Women members of the Seventh Day Adventist are the most hated under the current system because they refuse to go for dances on Saturday, We still call upon the MCP to respect the Sabbath and stop forcing women to attend to political matters on this day instead of worshipping God.
>
> SDA Woman, Chileka[50]

The Seventh Day Adventist Church presents a political attitude that does not fit into the categories of "prophetic voice" or "witness" as often applied to the classical churches. Its premises (esp. on church-state relationship) are fundamentally different. They may make them less vocal supporters of the process of change, but it also prevents them becoming enthusiastic supporters of a new political regime, as happened to the CCAP at independence. Therefore their voice should be heard in theological thinking.

7. Other Post–classical Churches

My information is insufficient to cover all the post–classical churches. Therefore I just want to mention a few things here. The Pentecostal churches, which elsewhere, for example in Latin America,

---

49 See: Felix Mponda, "SDA Church spells out its apolitical stance", *The New Express*, 11–17.6.1993.
50 *The Nation*, 11–17.6.1994.

are "the option of the poor"[51], do not seem to be prominent in that role here. But it should be recorded that two leaders in the process of transition are Pentecostals: Harry Chiume (Churches of Jesus Christ)[52] and Rev Dr Dumbo Lemani, who started his political carreer as Banda's first detainee and now is a member of the United Full Gospel Church.[53]

8. Owning and Disowning a (Post–classical) Hero

I close this paper with a look back into history. The post–classical missions can be proud of two men who, not without cost, resisted the oppressive political system of their time, Joseph Booth[54] and John Chilembwe[55]. Booth among other things wrote (in 1897!) a book called *Africa for the Africans*,[56] and Chilembwe led the 1915 Rising. Since *Africa for the Africans* is difficult to get, in Malawi as in the USA, it is understandable (and excusable) that the Ngwazi, despite his love for everything *Chizungu*, never claimed the Booth heritage for himself. But his attitude to Chilembwe and his heritage is more astonishing, and a number of questions remain unanswered, because the overall impression is that Banda both used the Chilembwe heritage and played it down at the same time. This is shown in the fact that he visited Providence Industrial Mission for the first and only time in the declining years of his political career. Dr. Malikebu, the successor of John Chilembwe, the Ngwazi honoured with his enmity. Rendell Day sheds some light on this issue:

> Dr. Malikebu had his disagreements with the President of
> Malawi, Dr. Hastings Kamuzu Banda and one such incident led

---

51 This term has been coined to challenge some churches' concept of their "preferential option *for* the poor".

52 According to other typologies it can be seen also as an African Independent Church.

53 *The Enquirer*, 19–25.10.1993. In this and following issues Lemani tells his story.

54 He is the founder of the following churches in Malawi: Zambezi Evangelical Church, Africa Evangelical Church, Church of Christ, Seventh Day Baptist Church, Seventh Day Adventist Church,

55 Chilembwe is the founder of the African Baptist Assembly, commonly known as Providence Industrial Mission.

56 Baltimore, 1897. A reprint is planned for 1994.

to the closing of the primary school at PIM. Rev. Chipuliko, the current Chairman of the PIM, gives two reasons for the closing of the school. First, Dr. Malikebu disagreed with the forced buying of "party" cards and second, Dr. Banda may have felt threatened by the strong leadership qualities that Dr. Malikebu had. Dr. Banda at one time called Dr. Malikebu a "capricorn" for he regarded him as a threat to his power. During Liberian President Tolbert's visit to Malawi, he insisted that Banda and Malikebu be reconciled. This seems to have helped to take off some of the pressure from Malikebu.[57]

With this historical background, it was understandable that UDF tried to claim the neglected heritage for itself, by rehabilitating the grave of some of the fallen heroes. With the church not being bound to one party, it was also logical that Rev. Chipuliko then invited all leaders (UDF, Aford, MCP) to a memorial celebration at Providence Industrial Mission.[58] The Ngwazi did not come, but the MCP was represented, and its representative felt obliged to outdo the opposition by donating not K 10000 to the Chilembwe scholarship fund, but by promising K 50000.[59] Feeling that this was not enough, he disclosed that the Ngwazi had generous plans for the development of the area, but he did not mention why the Ngwazi had needed 30 years to develop them.[60]

9. Conclusion

Though the contribution of the post–classical churches differed in many ways from that of the classical denominations, it was and is far from being negligible. It deserves attention as such, but also because of its different undergirding theological premises.

---

[57] Rendell Day, From Gowa Industrial Mission to Landmark Missionary Baptists, p. 10 (Int. with Rev. Chipuliko). Tolbert always was an active Baptist, for some time also a Vice-President of the Baptist World Alliance.
[58] The Monitor, 7.2.1994; The Mirror, 3.12.1993 (The Mirror shows the correct monument at Nsoni, the one in the Monitor was not erected by UDF).
[59] Even a week after the election, despite repeated promises to the contrary, the money had not been paid. UDF and AFORD have paid what they promised.
[60] A PIM member commented: "They haven't done anything for us for 30 years, should we be impressed with 50 000 Kwacha?"